Good Housekeeping

Vegetarian Meals

Meatless Recipes
Everyone Will Love

This custom edition published by
World Publications Group, Inc.
140 Laurel Street
East Bridgewater, MA 02333
www.wrldpub.com

Originally published by Hearst Books
in a different format as
*Vegetarian Meals Good Housekeeping
Favorite Recipes*

Book design by Renato Stanisic

Photography Credits
FRONT COVER Rita Maas
BACK COVER Mary Ellen Bartley
INTERIOR
Quentin Bacon 32
James Baigrie 137
Mary Ellen Bartley 117
Beatriz Da Costa 47, 60
Brian Hagiwara 6, 36, 48, 81, 86, 89, 90, 93,
94, 100, 103, 105, 106, 109, 112, 114, 118, 124,
129, 133, 134, 144, 146, 149, 155
Rita Maas 19, 138
Alan Richardson 3, 29, 68, 78, 83, 121, 130,
140, 152
Ann Stratton 4, 14, 21, 25, 26, 35, 41, 44, 53,
56, 65, 67
Mark Thomas 63, 75, 98, 150
Jonelle Weaver 8, 72

The Good Housekeeping Seal guarantees that
the recipes in this cookbook meet the strict
standards of the Good Housekeeping Research
Institute. The Institute has been a source of
reliable information and a consumer advocate
since 1900, and established its seal of approval in
1909. Every recipe has been triple-tested for
ease, reliability, and great taste.

Hearst Books
A division of Sterling Publishing Co., Inc.
387 Park Avenue South
New York, NY 10016

Good Housekeeping is a registered trademark
of Hearst Communications, Inc.

www.goodhousekeeping.com

Manufactured in China

ISBN 978-1-57215-623-4

10 9 8 7 6 5 4 3 2 1

Good Housekeeping

Vegetarian Meals

Meatless Recipes
Everyone Will Love

HEARST BOOKS
A division of Sterling Publishing Co., Inc.

New York / London
www.sterlingpublishing.com

Caribbean Black Bean Soup
recipe on page 20

CONTENTS

Spring Onion, Spinach, and
Pecorino Frittata
recipe on page 55

FOREWORD

I cook a lot of meatless dinners these days. Like many of you, I find that I'm not hungry for meat every night and I know that we get more than our fair share of protein. Growing up in an Italian-American family, a frittata, minestrone, and pasta e fagioli were often the main course at dinner, which might have been rounded out with cheese, along with a platter of broccoli drizzled with olive oil and lemon juice, or a simple tossed salad. I always loved these dinners but somehow never thought of them as "vegetarian."

Can a whole book on *Vegetarian Cooking* be real food for real families? Yes. Even if you have only 30 minutes to make dinner for picky eaters? Yes. This collection of over 150 recipes will give you family-friendly weeknight choices that require no mysterious ingredients or complicated techniques. Along with recipes there are tips, shortcuts, and suggestions for rounding out the meal, and some variations on featured recipes. You'll find chapters on Soups and Stews, Lunch and Brunch, Main-Dish Salads, Quick Dinners, and One-Dish Meals—so whatever you're cooking for, we've got you covered. And with these delicious triple-tested selections, we think you'll hear lots exclamations of "Yum!"

—Susan Westmoreland
Food Director, *Good Housekeeping*

Penne with Green Beans
and Basil
recipe on page 73

INTRODUCTION

For generations, the mealtime mantra of mothers across America has been "Eat your vegetables!" Well, as usual, mother is right. So too are the health professionals who, for decades, have advocated a healthy diet of less meat and more fruits, vegetables, whole grains, lowfat or fat-free dairy products to help us live longer and better.

Americans have finally gotten the message. Tens of millions of people in the U.S. today have changed their eating habits to include more produce and grains and fewer animal products.

While you may not consider yourself a vegetarian, you probably do, in fact, eat a few meatless meals each week. Pancakes for brunch, yogurt and fruit for breakfast, an after-movie pizza with mushrooms and peppers, a quick lunch of vegetable-and-bean burritos, comforting mac-and-cheese casserole or take-out vegetable lo mein for dinner are all satisfying and nutritious fare, yet free of meat, fish, or poultry.

TYPES OF VEGETARIANS

Vegetarians choose to eliminate animal products from their diets for any number of reasons—ethical, environmental, economic, or religious. But according to a recent Gallup Poll, the majority of people who choose to go meatless do so for health reasons. Vegetarians usually fall into one of these groups:

• The **vegan,** or **total vegetarian,** diet includes only foods from plant sources: fruits, vegetables, legumes (dried beans and peas), whole grains, seeds, and nuts.

- The **lactovegetarian** diet includes plant foods plus cheese and other dairy products.
- The **ovo-lactovegetarian** diet is the same as the lactovegetarian, but also includes eggs.
- The **semivegetarian** diet, which is frequently favored by those who are just easing into a vegetarian lifestyle or who want to add more meat-less meals to their diet, does not include red meat but does include chicken and fish along with plant foods, dairy products, and eggs.

EATING VEGETARIAN

Good Housekeeping does not advocate a vegetarian diet in *Vegetarian Meals.* Rather, we assembled a collection of our favorite healthful, flavor-packed recipes because, like many of our readers, you want to add more nutritious meatless dishes to your family's meals. Perhaps you have a member of your family who is a vegetarian, or your child has just announced that he or she wants to give up all animal foods. Or you simply want to introduce more vegetables, fruits, whole grains, legumes, and lowfat products into your meals. In these pages, you'll find a veritable garden of tasty, appealing, meat-free dishes to please everyone at your table.

Like life, variety is the key to delicious vegetarian meals. Experiment with the many available grains, legumes, fruits, and vegetables and combine them with several of the vast array of herbs and spices to marry flavors and add punch. You'll discover that the possibilities are endless.

NUTRITIONAL GUIDELINES

The most important consideration for a nutritionally sound vegetarian diet is to consume a variety of foods and in sufficient amounts to meet the caloric and nutritional needs of each individual. If you are incorporating more meatless meals into your family's menus and fewer animal products, there are several nutrients that you need to focus on to be sure everyone is getting an adequate amount, particularly youngsters:

Protein. You don't need to consume meat, fish, or poultry to have enough protein in your diet. Protein needs can easily be met by eating a variety of plant foods. It is not necessary to include specific combinations of foods (such as rice and beans) in the same meal. A mixture of proteins from grains, legumes, seeds, and vegetables eaten throughout the day will provide enough of all the amino acids, the building blocks of protein, your body needs.

Some sources of protein for vegetarians: legumes (dried peas and beans), seeds, nuts and nut butters, soy protein, cheese, milk and yogurt, eggs, grains, and some vegetables.

Iron. An integral part of hemoglobin which carries oxygen in the blood. Vegetarians who eliminate all meat, poultry and seafood (the primary sources of iron) may be prone to an iron deficiency.

Some sources of iron for vegetarians: legumes, dark green leafy vegetables (except spinach), enriched and whole-grain breads and cereals, nuts, and seeds. Cooking foods in cast-iron cookware can also boost their iron content.

Calcium: The major building material for building bones and teeth.

Some sources of calcium for vegetarians: milk and milk products, dark green leafy vegetables (except spinach), calcium-fortified soy products, fortified juices and cereals.

Zinc. Essential for growth and development and proper functioning of the immune system.

Some sources of zinc for vegetarians: legumes, wheat germ, whole grains, nuts, pumpkin and sunflower seeds, milk and milk products.

Vitamin B-12. Essential for formation of red blood cells and proper functioning of the nervous system. Animal products are the only natural food source of this vitamin.

Some sources of B-12 for vegetarians: milk and milk products, eggs, fortified foods and supplements.

THE VEGETARIAN FOOD GROUPS

Adopting a healthful vegetarian or semivegetarian diet is as simple as choosing a variety of different foods daily from among each of the following seven categories. Try any of the suggested recipes.

• **Breads and grains.** Choose whole or unrefined grain products whenever possible or use fortified or enriched cereals. *Recipes:* Wheat-Berry Salad with Spinach, Roasted Vegetables with Arugula and Whole-Wheat Fusili, Barley Vegetable Stew.

• **Vegetables and fruits.** Always try to use the freshest produce you can get. When fresh is not available, opt first for frozen, then canned. Go for the deepest colors for the highest nutritional content: Most dark green leafy vegetables contain calcium and iron. Deep yellow and orange fruits and vegetables are good sources of beta carotene. Veggies and fruits are also rich in potassium, fiber, folic acid, and vitamin C. *Recipes:* Eggplant and Spinach Stacks, Spiced Sweet-Potato Stew, Vegetarian Tortilla Pie.

- **Beans, peas, soy, and other legumes.** Use beans, peas, and other legumes as a main dish or part of a meal often. They are excellent sources of protein, and also contribute zinc, calcium, and iron. *Recipes:* White Bean and Tomatillo Chili, Lentil Shepherd's Pie, Falafel Sandwiches.

- **Dairy products or calcium-rich substitutes.** If using dairy products, select reduced-fat, lowfat, or fat-free varieties whenever possible. *Recipes:* Savory Rice and Ricotta Tart, Nacho Casserole, Eggplant Parmesan.

- **Nuts and seeds.** Eat a variety of nuts and seeds as a snack, on fruit or vegetable salads, or in main dishes. They are a source of protein, zinc, and iron. Don't overdo—they are high in calories.

- **Fats.** Essential in any diet, but ideally, most fats should come from whole plant foods such as nuts, seeds, and avocado. Moderate amounts of plant oils such as olive, canola, and sesame are good choices for cooking or for salad dressings.

- **Eggs.** Because of their high cholesterol content, you may want to limit eggs to three or four a week or consider using commercial egg substitutes, which contain no cholesterol and can be used freely as a protein source. *Recipes:* Leek and Goat Cheese Quiche, Spinach and Jack Cheese Bread Pudding, Mexican Potato Frittata.

PLANNING MEALS

The key to serving delicious vegetarian meals everyone will enjoy is to create dishes that include some of each food group and have a variety of tastes, colors, and textures.

If you're just beginning on the path to more meatless meals, you may find some resistance from the carnivores in your family. Understand that it will take some time for those who are used to thinking of vegetables as side dishes to see them as the main event. Ask everyone to contribute a list of his or her favorite foods. Many dishes that contain meat can be easily modified to make them vegetarian. Chili, stir-fries, and pasta dishes naturally lend themselves to meatless recipes.

In general, plan your meals around one main dish that is vegetable-, bean-, or grain-based. Then add the appropriate go-withs. For example, if your main course is a vegetable tart, accompany it with potato, grain, or corn for a nutritionally complete meal. With a main course of pasta, add a salad and whole-grain bread. A bean-and-vegetable casserole calls for a side of rice pilaf or other grain.

TIPS FOR BUSY PEOPLE

Most of us spend our days on the go: at work, shuttling kids back and forth, shopping, doing chores. Preparing good, wholesome vegetarian meals for your family shouldn't be a burden. Here are a few shortcuts for healthier cooking.

- Plan menus, make lists, then shop.
- Make sure there are plenty of good-quality ingredients on hand for quick and/or last-minute meals such as pastas, canned beans and tomatoes, frozen vegetables, and cheeses.
- Make two big casseroles or a double-batch of a one-pot dish that will feed your family for two nights. Serve with a salad and whole-grain bread.
- On the weekend, do some basic prep work of foods that can be incorporated into meals during the week: Cook up some rice or other grain, make pasta sauce, or cook a pot of beans.
- Get everyone involved in planning, shopping, and preparing meals. That way, they'll be more likely to eat and enjoy the meal. This approach is also a great way to get children started on healthy eating habits.

SOUPS AND STEWS

Curried Sweet-Potato and Lentil Soup
recipe on page 34

Stovetop Chili

A quick weeknight chili that's packed with buttery black soybeans, tender-crisp green beans, and melt-in-your-mouth sweet potatoes. Serve with a chunk of warm corn bread.

PREP: 20 MINUTES   COOK: 35 MINUTES
MAKES ABOUT 11 CUPS OR 6 MAIN-DISH SERVINGS.

1 tablespoon olive oil
1 medium onion, chopped
2 tablespoons chili powder
1 teaspoon ground cumin
1 teaspoon ground coriander
2 garlic cloves, crushed with
  garlic press
1 jalapeño chile, seeded and minced
1 can (28 ounces) whole tomatoes
1/2 pound green beans, trimmed and
  each cut crosswise in half

3 medium sweet potatoes (about
  1 1/2 pounds), peeled and cut
  into 1 1/2-inch pieces
1 teaspoon sugar
1 teaspoon salt
2 cups water
2 cans (15 ounces) black soybeans
  or black beans, rinsed and drained
sour cream (optional)

1. In nonstick 5- to 6-quart Dutch oven, heat oil over medium heat until hot. Add onion and cook, stirring occasionally, until tender, about 10 minutes. Add chili powder, cumin, coriander, garlic, and jalapeño; cook, stirring, 1 minute.

2. Add tomatoes with their juice, green beans, sweet potatoes, sugar, salt, and water; heat to boiling over medium-high heat, breaking up tomatoes with side of spoon. Reduce heat to low; cover and simmer, stirring occasionally, until sweet potatoes are tender, about 25 minutes.

3. Add soybeans and heat through, about 2 minutes longer. Serve with sour cream, if you like.

Each serving: About 275 calories, 14g protein, 45g carbohydrate, 5g total fat (1g saturated), 0mg cholesterol, 635mg sodium.

Cranberry Bean Soup

A Chilean-style soup made with butternut squash, tomatoes, fresh basil, and jalapeño. Cranberry beans have large, knobby beige pods speckled with red; the beans inside are cream-colored with red streaks and have a nutlike taste.

PREP: 40 MINUTES   COOK: 45 MINUTES
MAKES ABOUT 9 CUPS OR 4 MAIN-DISH SERVINGS.

4 teaspoons olive oil
1 medium butternut squash
  (2 pounds), peeled and cut into
  3/4-inch pieces
1 medium onion, chopped
2 garlic cloves, minced
1 jalapeño chile, seeded and minced
1 teaspoon ground cumin
1 can (14 1/2 ounces) vegetable broth
  (1 3/4 cups)

2 medium tomatoes, chopped
1 1/2 pounds fresh cranberry beans,
  shelled (about 2 cups beans)
1 teaspoon salt
1 teaspoon sugar
1 1/4 cups loosely packed fresh
  basil leaves, chopped
2 1/4 cups water
2 cups corn kernels cut from cobs
  (about 4 medium ears)

1. In 5-quart Dutch oven, heat 2 teaspoons oil over medium heat until hot. Add squash and onion and cook, stirring occasionally, until golden, about 10 minutes. Transfer squash mixture to bowl.

2. In same Dutch oven, heat remaining 2 teaspoons olive oil over medium heat; add garlic, jalapeño, and cumin and cook, stirring, 1 minute. Stir in broth, tomatoes, beans, salt, sugar, squash mixture, 1/4 cup basil, and water; heat to boiling over high heat. Reduce heat to low; cover and simmer, stirring occasionally, until beans are tender, about 30 minutes.

3. Stir in corn; heat to boiling over high heat. Reduce heat to low; cover and simmer 5 minutes longer. Stir in remaining 1 cup chopped basil.

Each serving: About 353 calories, 15g protein, 68g carbohydrate, 7g total fat (1g saturated), 0mg cholesterol, 854mg sodium.

Vegetarian Chili

Black soybeans, sold in convenient cans, have a better texture and flavor than the usual beige variety and add extra oomph to winter chili.

PREP: 30 MINUTES COOK: 50 MINUTES
MAKES ABOUT 10 CUPS OR 6 MAIN-DISH SERVINGS.

4 teaspoons olive oil
1 medium butternut squash (about 2 pounds), peeled and cut into 3/4-inch pieces
3 medium carrots, peeled and cut into 1/4-inch pieces
1 large onion (12 ounces), chopped
2 tablespoons chili powder
2 garlic cloves, crushed with garlic press

1 can (28 ounces) plum tomatoes
3 jalapeño chiles, seeded and minced
1 cup vegetable broth
1 tablespoon sugar
1/2 teaspoon salt
2 cans (15 ounces each) black soybeans, rinsed and drained
1 cup lightly packed fresh cilantro leaves, chopped
plain nonfat yogurt (optional)

1. In nonstick 5-quart Dutch oven or saucepot, heat 2 teaspoons oil over medium-high heat until hot. Add squash and cook, stirring occasionally, until golden, 8 to 10 minutes. Transfer squash to bowl; set aside.

2. In same Dutch oven, heat remaining 2 teaspoons oil. Add carrots and onion and cook, stirring occasionally, until golden, about 10 minutes. Stir in chili powder and garlic; cook, stirring, 1 minute longer.

3. Add tomatoes with their juice, jalapeños, broth, sugar, and salt; heat to boiling over medium-high heat, stirring to break up tomatoes with side of spoon. Stir in soybeans and squash; heat to boiling over medium-high heat. Reduce heat to low; cover and simmer until squash is tender, about 30 minutes.

4. Remove Dutch oven from heat; stir in cilantro. Serve chili with yogurt, if you like.

Each serving: About 265 calories, 15g protein, 40g carbohydrate, 6g total fat (1g saturated), 0mg cholesterol, 480mg sodium.

Vegetarian Chili

Caribbean Black Bean Soup

Our new take on black bean soup is made with allspice, thyme, and brown sugar for authentic island flair.

PREP: 45 MINUTES PLUS SOAKING BEANS   COOK: 2 HOURS 30 MINUTES
MAKES ABOUT 13 CUPS OR 6 MAIN-DISH SERVINGS.

1 pound dry black beans
2 tablespoons vegetable oil
2 medium red onions, chopped
4 jalapeño chiles, seeded and minced
2 tablespoons minced, peeled
   fresh ginger
4 garlic cloves, minced
1/2 teaspoon ground allspice
1/2 teaspoon dried thyme
8 cups water

2 medium sweet potatoes (about 12
   ounces each), peeled and cut into
   3/4-inch pieces
1 tablespoon dark brown sugar
2 teaspoons salt
1 bunch green onions, trimmed and
   thinly sliced
1 cup lightly packed fresh
   cilantro leaves, chopped
2 limes, cut into wedges (optional)

1. Place beans in colander and pick through, discarding any stones or debris. Rinse beans with cold running water and drain. Transfer beans to large bowl. Add enough *water* to cover by 2 inches. Cover and let stand at room temperature overnight. (Or, in 5-quart Dutch oven or saucepot, combine beans and enough *water* to cover by 2 inches; heat to boiling over high heat. Boil 2 minutes. Remove from heat; cover and let stand 1 hour.) Drain and rinse beans.

2. In 6-quart saucepot, heat vegetable oil over medium heat until hot. Add onions and cook, stirring occasionally, until tender, about 10 minutes. Add jalapeños, ginger, garlic, allspice, and thyme and cook, stirring, 3 minutes.

3. Add beans and water; heat to boiling over high heat. Reduce heat to low; cover and simmer 1 hour 30 minutes.

4. Add sweet potatoes, brown sugar, and salt; heat to boiling over high heat. Reduce heat to low; cover and simmer until beans and sweet potatoes are tender, about 30 minutes longer.

5. Transfer 1 cup bean mixture to blender; cover, with center part of cover removed to let steam escape, and puree until smooth. Return to saucepot. Stir in green onions and cilantro. Serve with lime wedges, if you like.

Each serving: About 390 calories, 17g protein, 70g carbohydrate, 6g total fat (1g saturated), 0mg cholesterol, 705mg sodium.

Caribbean Black Bean Soup

Vegetarian Lentil Stew

With ready-made soup as its base and precut squash, this hearty Indian-spiced stew is a breeze to prepare.

PREP: 10 MINUTES   COOK: 20 MINUTES
MAKES ABOUT 6 1/4 CUPS OR 4 MAIN-DISH SERVINGS.

2 teaspoons olive oil
2 teaspoons grated, peeled
   fresh ginger
2 garlic cloves, crushed with
   garlic press
2 teaspoons curry powder
1 package (1 pound) precut peeled
   butternut squash (about 4 cups),
   cut into bite-size pieces

1 large apple, unpeeled, cored,
   and cut into 1-inch pieces
1 can (19 ounces) ready-to-serve
   lentil soup
1/4 teaspoon salt
1 cup water
1 bag (10 ounces) prewashed
   spinach
lavash or pita, toasted (optional)

1. In 4-quart saucepan, heat oil over medium heat until hot. Add ginger, garlic, and curry powder, and cook, stirring, 30 seconds. Add squash, apple, soup, salt, and water; cover and heat to boiling over high heat. Reduce heat to medium; cook, covered, until squash is just tender, about 5 minutes longer, stirring occasionally.

2. In batches, gently add as many spinach leaves as will fit in the saucepan to lentil mixture, stirring until spinach has wilted. Cover and simmer gently 5 minutes. Serve stew with lavash, if you like.

Each serving: About 190 calories, 9g protein, 34g carbohydrate, 4g total fat (0g saturated), 0mg cholesterol, 650mg sodium.

Red Bean and Collard Gumbo

Gumbo is traditionally made with a variety of meats and shellfish, but you're not likely to be disappointed with this all-vegetable version.

PREP: 20 MINUTES   COOK: 30 MINUTES
MAKES ABOUT 8 CUPS OR 4 MAIN-DISH SERVINGS.

1/4 cup all-purpose flour
1 tablespoon olive oil
1 medium onion, thinly sliced
1 medium red pepper, cut into
   1/2-inch pieces
1 large stalk celery, thinly sliced
2 garlic cloves, crushed with
   garlic press
1/2 teaspoon salt
1/4 teaspoon ground red pepper
   (cayenne)

1/4 teaspoon dried thyme
1/4 teaspoon ground allspice
1 can (14 1/2 ounces) vegetable broth
   (1 3/4 cups)
3 cups water
1 bunch collard greens (about
   1 1/4 pounds), tough stems trimmed
   and leaves coarsely chopped
2 cans (15 to 19 ounces each) small
   red beans, rinsed and drained

1. In dry nonstick 5- to 6-quart saucepot, toast flour over medium heat, stirring frequently, until pale golden, about 5 minutes. Transfer flour to medium bowl; set aside.

2. In same saucepot, heat oil over medium-high heat until hot. Add onion, red pepper, and celery and cook, stirring occasionally, until vegetables are tender-crisp, about 10 minutes. Add garlic, salt, ground red pepper, thyme, and allspice and cook, stirring, 2 minutes.

3. Whisk broth into toasted flour until blended. Stir broth mixture and water into vegetables in saucepot; heat to boiling over medium-high heat. Add collard greens, stirring until wilted; stir in beans. Heat gumbo to boiling. Reduce heat to medium-low; cover and simmer until greens are tender, about 10 minutes.

Each serving: About 330 calories, 17g protein, 58g carbohydrate, 6g total fat (1g saturated), 0mg cholesterol, 1,190mg sodium.

Creamy Italian White Bean Soup

A perfect marriage of canned beans and fresh spinach, with a squeeze of fresh lemon juice for flavor.

PREP: 15 MINUTES   COOK: 40 MINUTES

MAKES ABOUT 6 CUPS OR 4 MAIN-DISH SERVINGS.

1 tablespoon vegetable oil
1 medium onion, finely chopped
1 medium stalk celery, finely chopped
1 garlic clove, minced
2 cans (15 1/2 to 19 ounces each)
   white kidney beans (cannellini),
   rinsed and drained
1 can (14 1/2 ounces) vegetable broth
   (1 3/4 cups)

1/4 teaspoon coarsely ground
   black pepper
1/8 teaspoon dried thyme
2 cups water
1 bunch (10 to 12 ounces) spinach
1 tablespoon fresh lemon juice
freshly grated Parmesan cheese
   (optional)

1. In 3-quart saucepan, heat oil over medium heat until hot. Add onion and celery and cook, stirring occasionally, until tender, 5 to 8 minutes. Add garlic; cook, stirring, 30 seconds. Add beans, broth, pepper, thyme, and water; heat to boiling over high heat. Reduce heat to low; simmer, uncovered, 15 minutes.

2. Meanwhile, trim tough stems from spinach and discard; thinly slice leaves.

3. With slotted spoon, remove 2 cups bean-and-vegetable mixture from soup; set aside. Spoon half of remaining mixture into blender; cover, with center part of cover removed to let steam escape, and puree until smooth. Pour into large bowl. Repeat with remaining mixture.

4. Return soup to saucepan; stir in reserved beans and vegetables. Heat to boiling over high heat, stirring occasionally. Stir in spinach and cook until wilted, about 1 minute. Stir in lemon juice and remove from heat. Serve with Parmesan, if you like.

Each serving without Parmesan: About 295 calories, 18g protein, 46g carbohydrate, 5g total fat (1g saturated), 0mg cholesterol, 945mg sodium.

Creamy Italian White Bean Soup

Tomato and Rice Soup

Tomato and Rice Soup

Serve this old-fashioned comfort food with crusty bread and a tossed salad for a satisfying winter meal. If you can't find either Wehani (an aromatic, reddish-brown rice that splits slightly when cooked and has a chewy texture) or black Japonica (a dark rice that tastes like a cross between basmati and wild rice), you can use long-grain brown rice.

PREP: 20 MINUTES   COOK: 50 MINUTES
MAKES ABOUT 7 1/2 CUPS OR 4 MAIN-DISH SERVINGS.

1/2 cup Wehani, black Japonica, or long-grain brown rice
1 tablespoon butter or margarine
1 medium onion, finely chopped
1 medium stalk celery, finely chopped
1 medium carrot, peeled and chopped
1 garlic clove, crushed with garlic press
1/4 teaspoon dried thyme
1 can (28 ounces) plum tomatoes in juice

1 can (14 1/2 ounces) vegetable broth (1 3/4 cups)
1/2 teaspoon salt
1/4 teaspoon coarsely ground black pepper
1 bay leaf
1 cup water
1/2 cup loosely packed fresh parsley leaves, chopped

1. Prepare rice as label directs but do not add salt or butter; set rice aside.

2. Meanwhile, in 4-quart saucepan, melt butter over medium heat. Add onion, celery, and carrot and cook, stirring occasionally, until tender, about 10 minutes. Stir in garlic and thyme; cook 1 minute.

3. Add tomatoes with their juice, broth, salt, pepper, bay leaf, and water; heat to boiling over high heat, breaking up tomatoes with side of spoon. Reduce heat to medium-low and cook, covered, 30 minutes. Discard bay leaf.

4. Spoon one-third of mixture into blender; cover, with center part of cover removed to let steam escape, and puree until almost smooth. Pour into large bowl. Repeat with remaining mixture.

5. Return soup to saucepan; heat over high heat until hot. Remove saucepan from heat; add cooked rice and chopped parsley.

Each serving: About 190 calories, 6g protein, 32g carbohydrate, 6g total fat (4g saturated), 8mg cholesterol, 960mg sodium.

Vegetable Soup with Bow Ties and Dill

Vegetable broth brimming with sautéed vegetables and tiny pasta bows is seasoned with a hint of lemon and lots of fresh dill—a perfect beginning to a light feast!

PREP: 25 MINUTES   COOK: 30 MINUTES
MAKES ABOUT 9 CUPS OR 4 MAIN-DISH SERVINGS.

1 lemon
1 tablespoon olive oil
1 large shallot, finely chopped
4 medium carrots, peeled and each cut lengthwise into quarters, then thinly sliced crosswise
2 medium stalks celery, thinly sliced

1 can (48 ounces) fat-free vegetable broth (6 cups)
1 cup water
1 package (10 ounces) frozen peas
3/4 cup small bow-tie pasta, cooked
3 tablespoons chopped fresh dill
1/8 teaspoon ground black pepper

1. From lemon, with vegetable peeler or small knife, remove 3" by 1" strip of peel; squeeze 1 tablespoon juice. Set aside.
2. In nonstick 5- to 6-quart saucepot, heat oil over medium-high heat until hot. Add shallot and cook, stirring frequently, until golden, about 2 minutes. Add carrots and celery and cook, stirring occasionally, until tender-crisp, about 5 minutes.
3. Add broth, lemon peel, and water; heat to boiling over medium-high heat. Reduce heat to low; cover and simmer until vegetables are tender, about 10 minutes.
4. Remove cover; stir in frozen peas and cook 1 minute longer. Stir in cooked pasta, dill, pepper, and lemon juice; heat through.

Each serving: About 240 calories, 10g protein, 34g carbohydrate, 4g total fat (2g saturated), 0mg cholesterol, 1540mg sodium.

Vegetable Soup with Bow Ties and Dill

Chilled Buttermilk-Vegetable Soup

The refreshing, cool flavors of summer vegetables make this chunky soup a delightful first course.

PREP: 20 MINUTES PLUS CHILLING
MAKES ABOUT 10 CUPS OR 6 MAIN-DISH SERVINGS.

2 limes
1½ quarts buttermilk (6 cups)
3 medium tomatoes (about 1 pound), seeded and cut into ¼-inch pieces
1 English (seedless) cucumber, unpeeled and cut into ¼-inch pieces
1 ripe avocado, cut into ¼-inch pieces

1 cup loosely packed fresh cilantro leaves, chopped
1 teaspoon salt
¼ teaspoon coarsely ground black pepper
cilantro sprigs for garnish

1. From limes, grate 1 teaspoon peel and squeeze 3 tablespoons juice.
2. In large bowl, combine lime peel and juice, buttermilk, tomatoes, cucumber, avocado, cilantro, salt, and pepper; stir until blended. Cover and refrigerate at least 2 hours or up to one day. Garnish each serving with a cilantro sprig.

Each serving: About 175 calories, 10g protein, 18g carbohydrate, 6g total fat (2g saturated), 8mg cholesterol, 632mg sodium.

Mushroom-Barley Miso Soup

Simmer shiitake mushrooms and barley in a miso broth. Never boil miso; its delicate flavor and nutrients will be destroyed by high heat.

PREP: 20 MINUTES   COOK: 1 HOUR

MAKES ABOUT 10 CUPS OR 6 MAIN-DISH SERVINGS.

1 package (1 ounce) dried shiitake mushrooms	$1/2$ cup pearl barley
1 tablespoon olive oil	$1/2$ teaspoon salt
3 medium carrots, peeled and cut into $1/4$-inch pieces	$1/4$ teaspoon coarsely ground black pepper
1 medium onion, chopped	$11/2$ pounds bok choy, trimmed and chopped
2 garlic cloves, minced	6 tablespoons dark red miso
1 tablespoon grated, peeled fresh ginger	1 tablespoon brown sugar

1. In 2-quart saucepan, heat *4 cups water* to boiling over high heat. Remove saucepan from heat; add dried shiitake mushrooms and let stand until softened, about 15 minutes. With slotted spoon, remove mushrooms. Rinse to remove any grit; drain on paper towels. Cut stems from mushrooms and discard; thinly slice caps. Strain soaking liquid through sieve lined with paper towels into 4-cup glass measuring cup. Add enough *water* to liquid in cup to equal 4 cups and set aside.

2. In nonstick 5-quart Dutch oven, heat oil over medium heat until hot. Add carrots, onion, and mushrooms and cook, stirring occasionally, until vegetables are tender, about 15 minutes. Add garlic and ginger and cook 1 minute longer.

3. Add barley, salt, pepper, reserved mushroom liquid, and an additional *4 cups water;* heat to boiling over medium-high heat. Reduce heat to low; cover and simmer until barley is tender, about 40 minutes.

4. Add bok choy; heat to boiling over medium-high heat. Reduce heat to low and simmer, uncovered, until bok choy is tender-crisp and wilted, 5 to 7 minutes, stirring occasionally.

5. With ladle, transfer $1/2$ cup broth from soup to small bowl. Add miso and brown sugar to broth and stir until smooth paste forms.

6. Remove Dutch oven from heat; stir in miso mixture.

Each serving: About 170 calories, 7g protein, 29g carbohydrate, 4g total fat (0g saturated), 0mg cholesterol, 985mg sodium.

Sweet-Potato and Peanut Stew

Sweet-Potato and Peanut Stew

A tasty vegetarian dish with tomatoes, warm spices, and a touch of creamy peanut butter. Microwaving the sweet potatoes helps you finish in a flash.

PREP: 15 MINUTES. COOK: 15 MINUTES
MAKES ABOUT 8 CUPS OR 4 MAIN-DISH SERVINGS.

3 medium sweet potatoes (about 12 ounces each), well scrubbed and cut into 1 1/2-inch pieces
1 tablespoon olive oil
2 garlic cloves, crushed with garlic press
1 1/2 teaspoons ground cumin
1/2 teaspoon salt
1/4 teaspoon ground cinnamon
1/8 teaspoon crushed red pepper
2 cans (15 to 19 ounces each) garbanzo beans, rinsed and drained
1 can (14 1/2 ounces) vegetable broth (1 3/4 cups)
1 can (14 1/2 ounces) diced tomatoes
1/4 cup creamy peanut butter
1/2 cup loosely packed fresh cilantro leaves, chopped

1. Place potatoes in 2 1/2-quart microwave-safe dish. Cover dish and microwave on High until fork-tender, about 8 minutes.

2. Meanwhile, in 5- to 6-quart saucepot, heat oil over medium-high heat until hot. Add garlic, cumin, salt, cinnamon, and crushed red pepper and cook, stirring, 30 seconds. Stir in beans, broth, tomatoes, and peanut butter until blended; heat to boiling and cook, stirring occasionally, 1 minute.

3. Reduce heat to medium-low; add sweet potatoes and simmer, stirring occasionally, 2 minutes. Stir in cilantro.

Each serving: About 585 calories, 22g protein, 92g carbohydrate, 16g total fat (2g saturated), 0mg cholesterol, 1,725mg sodium.

Curried Sweet-Potato and Lentil Soup

This thick and hearty soup is packed with spicy flavor. Get it going, then call a friend or spend some time with the kids while it simmers.

PREP: 15 MINUTES   COOK: 1 HOUR 15 MINUTES
MAKES ABOUT 14 CUPS OR 8 MAIN-DISH SERVINGS.

2 tablespoons butter or margarine
2 medium sweet potatoes (about
   12 ounces each), peeled and cut
   into 1/2-inch chunks
2 large stalks celery, cut into
   1/4-inch pieces
1 large onion (12 ounces), cut into
   1/4-inch pieces
1 garlic clove, minced
1 tablespoon curry powder
1 tablespoon grated, peeled
   fresh ginger

1 teaspoon ground cumin
1 teaspoon ground coriander
1 teaspoon salt
1/8 teaspoon ground red pepper
   (cayenne)
2 cans (14 1/2 ounces each)
   vegetable broth (3 1/2 cups)
1 package (16 ounces) dry lentils,
   rinsed and picked through
6 cups water
yogurt, toasted coconut, and lime
   wedges (optional)

1. In 6-quart Dutch oven, melt butter over medium heat. Add the sweet potatoes, celery, and onion and cook, stirring occasionally, until onion is tender, about 10 minutes. Add garlic, curry powder, ginger, cumin, coriander, salt, and ground red pepper; cook, stirring, 1 minute.

2. To vegetables in Dutch oven, add broth, lentils, and water; heat to boiling over high heat. Reduce heat to low; cover and simmer, stirring occasionally, until lentils are tender, 40 to 45 minutes. Serve with yogurt, toasted coconut, and lime wedges, if you like.

Each serving without yogurt, coconut, and lime: About 295 calories, 15g protein, 15g carbohydrate, 5g total fat (2g saturated), 8mg cholesterol, 646mg sodium.

Curried Sweet-Potato and Lentil Soup

Carrot and Apple Soup

Carrot and Apple Soup

If you own a hand blender, you can puree this winning combination of sweet carrots and apples right in the Dutch oven. We call for Golden Delicious apples for their consistently good flavor, but feel free to substitute other varieties.

PREP: 20 MINUTES   COOK: 35 MINUTES
MAKES ABOUT 10 CUPS OR 6 MAIN-DISH SERVINGS.

2 tablespoons butter or margarine
1 large onion (12 ounces), coarsely chopped
3 medium Golden Delicious apples
2 pounds carrots
2 cans (14 1/2 ounces each) vegetable broth
1 tablespoon sugar

1 teaspoon salt
1 teaspoon grated, peeled fresh ginger
2 cups water
half-and-half or heavy cream for garnish (optional)
fresh chives for garnish

1. In 5-quart Dutch oven, melt butter over medium heat. Add onion and cook, stirring occasionally, until tender and golden, about 12 minutes.

2. Meanwhile, peel apples and carrots. Cut each apple in half and remove core. Cut apples and carrots into 1 1/2-inch chunks.

3. Add apples, carrots, broth, sugar, salt, ginger, and water to onion; heat to boiling over high heat. Reduce heat to low; cover and simmer until carrots are very tender, about 20 minutes.

4. Remove Dutch oven from heat. Spoon one third of mixture into blender; cover, with center part of cover removed to let steam escape, and puree until very smooth.

5. Return soup to Dutch oven; heat through. Serve soup with a swirl of half-and-half, if you like. Garnish with fresh chives.

Each serving: About 173 calories, 3g protein, 30g carbohydrate, 7g total fat (3g saturated), 10mg cholesterol, 1,022mg sodium.

Broccoli and Cheddar Soup

For a satisfying meal, serve this rich soup with an artisinal multigrain bread and a crisp salad. Use a blender—not a food processor—for an extrasmooth texture.

PREP: 35 MINUTES   COOK: 25 MINUTES
MAKES ABOUT 8 CUPS OR 4 MAIN-DISH SERVINGS.

1 tablespoon olive oil
1 medium onion, chopped
1/4 cup all-purpose flour
1/2 teaspoon salt
1/4 teaspoon dried thyme
1/8 teaspoon ground nutmeg
coarsely ground black pepper
2 cups reduced-fat milk (2%)
1 can (14 1/2 ounces) vegetable broth
  (1 3/4 cups)

1 1/2 cups water
1 large bunch (1 1/2 pounds) broccoli, trimmed and cut into 1-inch pieces (including stems)
1 1/2 cups shredded sharp Cheddar cheese (6 ounces)
coarsely ground black pepper

1. In 4-quart saucepan, heat oil over medium heat until hot. Add onion and cook, stirring occasionally, until golden, about 10 minutes. Stir in flour, salt, thyme, nutmeg, and 1/4 teaspoon pepper; cook, stirring frequently, 2 minutes.

2. Gradually stir in milk, broth, and water. Add broccoli and heat to boiling over high heat. Reduce heat to low; cover and simmer until broccoli is tender, about 10 minutes.

3. Spoon one-third of mixture into blender; cover, with center part of cover removed to let steam escape, and puree until very smooth. Pour into large bowl. Repeat with remaining batches.

4. Return the soup to saucepan; heat to boiling over high heat, stirring occasionally. Remove saucepan from heat; stir in cheese until melted and smooth. Sprinkle each serving with coarsely ground black pepper.

Each serving: About 362 calories, 24g protein, 26g carbohydrate, 22g total fat (12g saturated), 52mg cholesterol, 934mg sodium.

Chunky Vegetable Chowder

Using an assortment of favorite fall vegetables in this hearty soup makes it a tasty and healthful comfort food.

PREP: 20 MINUTES   COOK: 30 MINUTES
MAKES ABOUT 13 CUPS OR 6 MAIN-DISH SERVINGS.

2 tablespoons olive oil

1 jumbo onion (1 pound), cut into 1/4-inch pieces

12 ounces red potatoes, unpeeled and cut into 1/2-inch pieces

3 medium carrots, peeled and cut into 1/4-inch pieces

2 medium parsnips (about 8 ounces), peeled and cut into 1/4-inch pieces

2 medium stalks celery, cut into 1/4-inch pieces

2 garlic cloves, crushed with garlic press

1 can (14 1/2 ounces) vegetable broth (1 3/4 cups)

3/4 teaspoon salt

1/4 teaspoon dried thyme

4 1/2 cups water

1 package (10 ounces) frozen Fordhook lima beans

12 ounces escarole or Swiss chard, trimmed and coarsely chopped

1. In nonstick 5- to 6-quart saucepot or Dutch oven, heat oil over medium-high heat until very hot. Add onion, potatoes, carrots, parsnips, celery, and garlic and cook, stirring occasionally, until vegetables are lightly browned, 15 minutes.

2. Add broth, salt, thyme, and water; heat to boiling over medium-high heat. Stir in lima beans and escarole; heat to boiling. Reduce heat to low; cover and simmer until vegetables are tender, about 10 minutes.

Each serving: About 220 calories, 7g protein, 39g carbohydrate, 5g total fat (1g saturated), 0mg cholesterol, 675mg sodium.

French Onion Soup

Slowly cooked onions add great, caramelized flavor to this classic. If you double the recipe, be sure to cook the onions in two skillets.

PREP: 15 MINUTES   COOK/BAKE: 1 HOUR 50 MINUTES
MAKES 6 1/2 CUPS OR 4 MAIN-DISH SERVINGS.

3 tablespoons butter or margarine
7 medium onions (about 2 1/2
    pounds), each cut lengthwise in
    half and thinly sliced
1/4 teaspoon salt
4 cups water

1 can (14 1/2 ounces) vegetable broth
    (1 3/4 cups)
1/4 teaspoon dried thyme
4 slices (1/2 inch thick) French bread
4 ounces Gruyère or Swiss cheese,
    shredded (1 cup)

1. In 12-inch skillet, melt butter over medium heat. Add onions and salt and cook, stirring occasionally, until onions are very tender and begin to caramelize, about 45 minutes. Reduce heat to low; cook, stirring often, until onions are deep golden brown, about 15 minutes longer.

2. Transfer onions to 3-quart saucepan. Add 1/2 cup water to skillet; heat to boiling over high heat, stirring until browned bits are loosened from bottom of pan. Pour into saucepan with onions. Add broth, thyme, and remaining water; heat to boiling over high heat. Reduce heat to low; cover and simmer until onions are very tender, about 30 minutes.

3. Meanwhile, preheat oven to 450°F. Place bread slices on small cookie sheet; bake until lightly toasted, about 5 minutes.

4. Place four 2 1/2-cup oven-safe bowls in 15 1/2" by 10 1/2" jelly-roll pan. Spoon onion soup into bowls; top with toasted bread, pressing toast lightly into soup. Sprinkle toast with cheese. Bake until cheese melts and begins to brown, 12 to 15 minutes.

Each serving: About 375 calories, 15g protein, 38g carbohydrate, 23g total fat (11g saturated), 54mg cholesterol, 808mg sodium.

French Onion Soup

Hot and Sour Soup

We streamlined seasonings to help get this popular Asian soup on the table in record time—without sacrificing the great taste.

PREP: 10 MINUTES: COOK: 20 MINUTES

MAKES ABOUT 8 CUPS OR 4 MAIN-DISH SERVINGS.

1 tablespoon vegetable oil

4 ounces shiitake mushrooms, stems removed and caps thinly sliced

3 tablespoons reduced-sodium soy sauce

1 package (15 to 16 ounces) extrafirm tofu, drained, patted dry, and cut into 1-inch cubes

2 tablespoons cornstarch

1 container (32 ounces) vegetable broth (4 cups)

3 tablespoons seasoned rice vinegar

2 tablespoons grated, peeled fresh ginger

1 tablespoon Worcestershire sauce

1/2 teaspoon Asian sesame oil

1/4 teaspoon ground red pepper (cayenne)

2 large eggs, beaten

2 green onions, trimmed and sliced

1. In nonstick 5-quart saucepot, heat vegetable oil over medium-high heat until hot. Add mushrooms, soy sauce, and tofu and cook, gently stirring often, until liquid has evaporated, about 5 minutes.

2. In cup, with fork, blend cornstarch and *1/4 cup water* until smooth; set aside. Add broth and *3/4 cup water* to tofu mixture; heat to boiling. Stir in cornstarch mixture and boil, stirring, 30 seconds. Reduce heat to medium-low; add vinegar, ginger, Worcestershire, sesame oil, and pepper and simmer 5 minutes.

3. Remove saucepot from heat. In a thin, steady stream, slowly pour beaten eggs into soup around side of saucepot. Carefully stir soup once in circular motion to separate egg into strands. Sprinkle with green onions.

Each serving: About 280 calories, 18g protein, 17g carbohydrate, 15g total fat (3g saturated), 106mg cholesterol, 1,790mg sodium.

Tip

To brown, tofu should be dry. Wrap in paper towels and set it on a plate. Cover with a second plate; place a heavy can on top and let drain fifteen minutes. Discard towels.

Harvest Mexican Soup

This soup is full of savory ingredients, including corn, avocado, and lime; a jalapeño chile adds a burst of heat.

PREP: 25 MINUTES   COOK: 30 MINUTES
MAKES ABOUT 9 1/2 CUPS OR 4 MAIN-DISH SERVINGS.

4 teaspoons olive oil
1 jumbo onion (1 pound), cut into
  1/4-inch pieces
2 medium carrots, peeled and cut
  into 1/4-inch pieces
2 garlic cloves, crushed with
  garlic press
1 jalapeño chile, seeded and minced
3 limes
12 ounces red potatoes, unpeeled
  and cut into 1/4-inch pieces

1 can (14 1/2 ounces) vegetable broth
  (1 3/4 cups)
1/2 teaspoon salt
4 cups water
2 cups corn kernels cut from cobs
  (3 to 4 ears)
1 cup loosely packed fresh cilantro
  leaves, chopped
1 avocado, cut into 1/4-inch pieces
plain tortilla chips, coarsely broken
  (optional)

1. In nonstick 5- to 6-quart saucepot or Dutch oven, heat oil over medium-high heat until hot. Add onion, carrots, garlic, and jalapeño, and cook, stirring occasionally, until vegetables are golden, 15 minutes.
2. Meanwhile, from limes, grate 1/2 teaspoon peel and squeeze 1/3 cup juice; set aside.
3. Add potatoes, broth, salt, and water to saucepot; heat to boiling over medium-high heat. Reduce heat to low; cover and simmer 5 minutes. Add corn; cover and simmer until potatoes are tender, about 5 minutes.
4. Stir in cilantro, lime peel, and lime juice. Ladle soup into 4 bowls; top with avocado and sprinkle with tortilla chips, if you like.

Each serving: About 350 calories, 8g protein, 58g carbohydrate, 14g total fat (2g saturated), 0mg cholesterol, 945mg sodium.

LUNCH AND BRUNCH

French Potato Pancake
recipe on page 64

Greek Salad Pitas

Hummus—the Middle Eastern spread made with mashed garbanzo beans—is fast work in a food processor or blender.

PREP: 20 MINUTES
MAKES 4 SANDWICHES.

1 can (15 to 19 ounces) garbanzo
  beans, rinsed and drained
1/4 cup plain lowfat yogurt
2 tablespoons olive oil
2 tablespoons fresh lemon juice
1/2 teaspoon salt
1/4 teaspoon coarsely ground
  black pepper
1/4 teaspoon ground cumin
1 garlic clove, peeled
4 (6- to 7-inch) whole-wheat pitas

3 cups sliced romaine lettuce
2 medium tomatoes, cut into
  1/4-inch pieces
1 medium cucumber, peeled and
  thinly sliced
2 ounces feta cheese, crumbled
  (about 1/2 cup)
2 tablespoons chopped fresh
  mint leaves
fresh mint leaves for garnish

1. In food processor, with knife blade attached, or in blender, combine beans, yogurt, oil, lemon juice, salt, pepper, cumin, and garlic and puree until smooth.

2. Cut off top third of each pita to form pocket. Use half of the bean mixture to spread inside pockets.

3. Combine lettuce, tomatoes, cucumber, feta, and chopped mint; use to fill pockets. Top with remaining bean mixture and mint leaves.

Each sandwich: About 440 calories, 17g protein, 66g carbohydrate, 15g total fat (4g saturated), 13mg cholesterol, 1,105mg sodium.

Greek Salad Pitas

Cream Cheese and Chive Scrambled Eggs

Cream Cheese and Chive Scrambled Eggs

Serve this versatile dish for a formal brunch or for a late-night family supper. A salad on the side rounds out the meal.

PREP: 5 MINUTES   COOK: 5 MINUTES
MAKES 4 MAIN-DISH SERVINGS.

1 bag (5 ounces) baby mixed salad
  greens
1 tablespoon olive oil
2 teaspoons red wine vinegar
pinch plus 1/2 teaspoon salt
8 large eggs
2 tablespoons chopped fresh chives
1/4 teaspoon coarsely ground black
  pepper

1/4 cup water
2 teaspoons butter or margarine
4 ounces (half 8-ounce package)
  Neufchâtel or light cream cheese,
  cut into 1/2-inch pieces
4 slices multigrain bread, toasted and
  each cut diagonally in half

1. In medium bowl, toss greens with oil, vinegar, and pinch salt; set aside.
2. In large bowl, with wire whisk, beat eggs, chives, pepper, remaining 1/2 teaspoon salt, and water until blended.
3. In nonstick 10-inch skillet, melt butter over medium-high heat; add egg mixture. With heat-safe rubber spatula, gently push egg mixture as it begins to set to form soft curds. When eggs are partially cooked, top with Neufchâtel and continue cooking, stirring occasionally, until eggs have thickened and no visible liquid egg remains.
4. To serve, divide greens among 4 dinner plates. Place 2 toast halves on each plate; spoon eggs over toast.

Each serving: About 340 calories, 18g protein, 15g carbohydrate, 24g total fat (9g saturated), 451mg cholesterol, 716mg sodium.

Leek and Goat Cheese Quiche

Meltingly tender sweet leeks and tangy goat cheese are delicious partners in this rich tart.

PREP: 30 MINUTES PLUS CHILLING AND COOLING   BAKE: 60 MINUTES
MAKES 8 MAIN-DISH SERVINGS.

Pastry for 11-inch tart (recipe follows)

FILLING

1 pound leeks (about 3 medium)
2 tablespoons butter or margarine
1/2 teaspoon salt
1/2 cup water
3 large eggs

1 log (3 1/2 to 4 ounces) mild goat cheese such as Montrachet
1/8 teaspoon ground black pepper
1 1/2 cups half-and-half or light cream

1. Prepare Pastry for 11-inch Tart as recipe directs.
2. On lightly floured surface, with floured rolling pin, roll dough into 14-inch round. Ease dough into 11" by 1" round tart pan with removable bottom. Fold overhang in and press dough against side of pan so it extends 1/8 inch above rim. With fork, prick dough at 1-inch intervals. Refrigerate 30 minutes or freeze 10 minutes. Preheat oven to 425°F.
3. Line tart shell with foil; fill with pie weights or dry beans. Bake 10 minutes. Remove foil with weights; bake until lightly golden, about 10 minutes longer. (If pastry puffs up during baking, gently press down with back of spoon.) Cool in pan on wire rack 20 minutes. Turn oven control to 350°F.
4. While tart shell bakes and cools, prepare filling: Cut off roots and trim dark green tops from leeks. Cut each leek lengthwise in half, then crosswise into 1/2-inch-thick slices. Rinse leeks in large bowl of cold water, swishing to remove sand; transfer to colander to drain, leaving sand in bottom of bowl.
5. In 12-inch skillet, melt butter over medium heat. Add leeks, 1/4 teaspoon salt, and water; cook, uncovered, until leeks are tender and all liquid has evaporated, about 10 minutes, stirring occasionally. Remove skillet from heat.
6. In medium bowl, with wire whisk, beat eggs, goat cheese, pepper, and remaining 1/4 teaspoon salt until well blended. Stir in half-and-half.

7. Place tart pan on foil-lined cookie sheet to catch any overflow. Sprinkle leeks over bottom of tart shell; pour egg mixture over leeks. Bake until knife inserted in center comes out clean, 35 to 40 minutes. Cool on wire rack 10 minutes. Just before serving, remove side of pan. Serve hot or at room temperature.

Each serving: About 410 calories, 10g protein, 26g carbohydrate, 31g total fat (17g saturated), 149mg cholesterol, 551mg sodium.

Pastry for 11-inch Tart

PREP: 10 MINUTES PLUS CHILLING
MAKES ONE 11-INCH TART SHELL.

1¹/₂ cups all-purpose flour
¹/₂ teaspoon salt
¹/₂ cup cold butter or margarine
**   (1 stick), cut into pieces**

2 tablespoons vegetable shortening
3 to 4 tablespoons ice water

1. In large bowl, mix flour and salt. With pastry blender or two knives used scissor-fashion, cut in butter and shortening until mixture resembles coarse crumbs.

2. Sprinkle in ice water, 1 tablespoon at a time, mixing lightly with fork after each addition, until dough is just moist enough to hold together. Shape dough into disk; wrap disk in plastic wrap. Refrigerate 30 minutes or up to overnight. (If chilled overnight, let stand 30 minutes at room temperature before rolling.)

Each ¹/₈ pastry: About 222 calories, 3g protein, 20g carbohydrate, 15g total fat (8g saturated), 32mg cholesterol, 263mg sodium.

Asparagus Omelet

If you don't have pale yellow, nutty-flavored Gruyère cheese, substitute the same amount of shredded Swiss or Jarlsberg, or a few shavings of fresh Parmesan.

PREP: 10 MINUTES   COOK: 5 MINUTES
MAKES 4 MAIN-DISH SERVINGS.

FILLING

1 pound asparagus, trimmed
1/8 teaspoon coarsely ground black pepper
4 ounces Gruyère cheese, shredded (1 cup)

OMELETS

8 large eggs (see Tip below)
1/2 teaspoon salt
1/2 cup cold water
4 teaspoons butter or margarine

1. Prepare filling: In deep 12-inch skillet, heat *1 inch water* to boiling over high heat. Add asparagus; heat to boiling. Reduce heat and simmer, uncovered, just until tender, about 5 minutes. Drain and rinse with cold running water. Drain. Sprinkle pepper over cheese.

2. To make omelets: In medium bowl, with wire whisk, beat eggs, salt, and cold water. For each omelet, in nonstick 8-inch skillet, melt 1 teaspoon butter over medium-high heat. Pour in 1/2 cup egg mixture; cook, gently lifting edge of eggs with heat-safe rubber spatula and tilting pan to allow uncooked eggs to run underneath, until eggs are set, about 1 minute. Sprinkle one-fourth of cheese mixture over half of omelet; top with one-fourth of asparagus spears. Fold unfilled half over filling and slide onto warm plate. Repeat with remaining butter, egg mixture, and filling. If desired, keep omelets warm in 200°F oven until all are cooked.

Each omelet: About 310 calories, 23g protein, 3g carbohydrate, 25g total fat (11g saturated), 467mg cholesterol, 528mg sodium.

Tip
For lighter omelets, substitute 4 large eggs and 8 large egg whites for the whole eggs.

Asparagus Omelet

Greens and Ricotta Pie

It's like a quiche without the crust! Swiss chard and green onion make up this savory dish—an easy entrée for lunch or brunch.

PREP: 30 MINUTES   BAKE: 40 MINUTES
MAKES 6 MAIN-DISH SERVINGS.

1 large head Swiss chard (about 1 3/4 pounds)
1 tablespoon olive oil
1 bunch green onions, cut into 1/4-inch-thick pieces
1/2 teaspoon salt
1/4 teaspoon coarsely ground black pepper

4 large eggs
1 container (15 ounces) part-skim ricotta cheese
3/4 cup low-fat milk (1%)
1/2 cup freshly grated Parmesan cheese
2 tablespoons cornstarch

1. Preheat oven to 350°F. Grease 9 1/2-inch deep-dish glass pie plate.

2. Trim off 2 inches from Swiss-chard stems; discard ends. Separate stems from leaves; thinly slice stems and coarsely chop leaves.

3. In nonstick 12-inch skillet, heat oil over medium-high heat until hot. Add sliced stems and cook, stirring frequently, until tender and lightly browned, about 4 minutes. Add green onions, salt, and pepper and cook 1 minute. Gradually add chopped leaves and cook, stirring, until leaves have wilted and excess moisture has evaporated, about 5 minutes.

4. In large bowl, with wire whisk, beat eggs, ricotta, milk, Parmesan, and cornstarch. Stir in Swiss-chard mixture.

5. Place prepared pie plate on foil-lined cookie sheet to catch any overflow. Pour mixture into pie plate. Bake pie until knife inserted 2 inches from center comes out clean, about 40 minutes.

Each serving: About 255 calories, 19g protein, 14g carbohydrate, 14g total fat (7g saturated), 172mg cholesterol, 680mg sodium.

Spring Onion, Spinach, and Pecorino Frittata

For a less assertive flavor, substitute Parmigiano-Reggiano for the Pecorino Romano or use a combination of the two for a more complex flavor.

PREP: 30 MINUTES   BAKE: 10 MINUTES
MAKES 4 MAIN-DISH SERVINGS.

- 2 spring onions with tops (about 12 ounces), or 1 large (12 ounces) sweet onion
- 2 teaspoons olive oil
- 1 bag (5 to 6 ounces) baby spinach
- 8 large eggs
- 1/4 cup freshly grated Pecorino Romano cheese
- 1/4 cup water
- 1/2 teaspoon salt
- 1/4 teaspoon coarsely ground black pepper

1. Preheat oven to 425°F. Trim tough green leaves from top of spring onions. Cut stems crosswise into 1/4-inch-thick slices. Cut each onion bulb in half and thinly slice.

2. In oven-safe nonstick 12-inch skillet (if skillet is not oven-safe, wrap handle with double layer of foil), heat oil over medium heat until hot. Add sliced onions and stems and cook, stirring occasionally, until soft and golden brown, about 10 minutes. Stir in spinach and cook, stirring constantly, just until wilted, about 1 minute. Spread onion mixture evenly in skillet; remove skillet from heat.

3. In medium bowl with wire whisk, beat eggs, Pecorino Romano, water, salt, and pepper until blended. Carefully pour egg mixture over onion mixture; do not stir. Return skillet to medium-high heat and cook until egg mixture begins to set around the edge, 2 to 3 minutes.

4. Place skillet in oven; bake until frittata is set, 8 to 10 minutes. Slide frittata onto cutting board. Cut into wedges to serve.

Each serving: About 215 calories, 16g protein, 7g carbohydrate, 14g total fat (4g saturated), 430mg cholesterol, 530mg sodium.

Spinach Strata

Spinach Strata

You can assemble this a day ahead, then pop it in the oven—right from the refrigerator—just one hour before serving.

PREP: 15 MINUTES PLUS CHILLING   BAKE: 1 HOUR
MAKES 6 MAIN-DISH SERVINGS.

8 slices firm white bread
4 ounces mozzarella cheese, shredded (1 cup)
1 package (10 ounces) frozen chopped spinach, thawed and squeezed dry
1 tablespoon butter or margarine, softened

2 cups milk
6 large eggs
1/2 cup loosely packed fresh basil leaves, chopped
1/2 teaspoon salt
1/4 teaspoon ground black pepper

1. Grease 8" by 8" glass baking dish. Place 4 bread slices in dish; top with 1/2 cup cheese, all spinach, then remaining cheese. Spread butter on 1 side of each remaining bread slice; place in dish, buttered side up.

2. In medium bowl, with wire whisk, beat milk, eggs, basil, salt, and pepper until blended. Slowly pour egg mixture over bread slices. Prick bread with fork and press slices down to absorb egg mixture. Cover baking dish with plastic wrap and refrigerate at least 30 minutes or overnight.

3. Preheat oven to 350°F. Remove cover from baking dish; bake strata until knife inserted in center comes out clean, about 1 hour. Remove from oven and let stand 5 minutes before serving.

Each serving: About 290 calories, 17g protein, 22g carbohydrate, 16g total fat (7g saturated), 245mg cholesterol, 569mg sodium.

Summer Squash and Potato Frittata with Sage

It takes just a few teaspoons of minced sage to jazz up a humble egg entrée—we love it for brunch or supper.

PREP: 50 MINUTES   BAKE: 15 MINUTES
MAKES 6 MAIN-DISH SERVINGS.

1 large all-purpose potato (8 ounces), peeled and cut into 1/2-inch pieces

1 1/2 teaspoons salt

2 tablespoons butter or margarine

1 medium red onion, thinly sliced

2 garlic cloves, minced

1 small yellow summer squash (about 4 ounces), cut into 2" by 1/4" strips

1 small zucchini (about 4 ounces), cut into 2" by 1/4" strips

2 teaspoons minced fresh sage leaves

1/4 teaspoon coarsely ground black pepper

8 large eggs

2 teaspoons balsamic vinegar

1. Preheat oven to 350°F. In 2-quart saucepan, combine potato, 1/2 teaspoon salt, and *enough water to cover*; heat to boiling over high heat. Reduce heat to low; cover and simmer until tender, about 10 minutes. Drain.

2. Meanwhile, in oven-safe nonstick 10-inch skillet (if skillet is not oven-safe, wrap handle with double layer of foil), melt butter over medium heat. Add onion and cook, stirring occasionally, until very soft, about 12 minutes.

3. Stir in the garlic; cook 1 minute. Add cooked potato, yellow squash, zucchini, sage, pepper, and remaining 1 teaspoon salt and cook, stirring occasionally, until zucchini is tender and liquid has evaporated, about 12 minutes.

4. In medium bowl, with wire whisk, beat eggs and vinegar. Pour egg mixture over vegetables in skillet and cook, covered, over medium heat until mixture begins to set around edge, about 3 minutes.

5. Remove cover and place skillet in oven; bake until frittata is set, about 15 minutes. Cut into wedges to serve.

Each serving: About 180 calories, 10g protein, 11g carbohydrate, 13g total fat (5g saturated), 294mg cholesterol, 528mg sodium.

Puffy Cheese Grits

Grits are a breakfast tradition throughout the South, where it is served with a pat of melting butter or a spoonful of redeye gravy (made by adding coffee to the skillet a ham steak was fried in). Southerners have perfected grits by baking them with plenty of cheese until they're hot and puffy, making this a dish enjoyed by all—whether you grew up eating grits or not.

PREP: 20 MINUTES   BAKE: 45 MINUTES
MAKES 8 MAIN-DISH SERVINGS.

3 1/2 cups milk
2 cups water
2 tablespoons butter or margarine
1 teaspoon salt
1 1/4 cups quick hominy grits

8 ounces Cheddar cheese, shredded (2 cups)
5 large eggs
1 teaspoon hot pepper sauce
1/4 teaspoon ground black pepper

1. Preheat oven to 325°F. Lightly grease shallow 2 1/2-quart casserole.

2. In 3-quart saucepan, combine 1 1/2 cups milk, water, butter, and salt; heat to boiling over medium-high heat. With wire whisk, gradually stir in grits, constantly beating to prevent lumps. Reduce heat; cover and cook, stirring occasionally with a wooden spoon, 5 minutes (grits will be very stiff). Remove from heat and stir in Cheddar.

3. In large bowl, with wire whisk, beat eggs, remaining 2 cups milk, hot pepper sauce, and black pepper until blended. Gradually stir grits mixture into egg mixture until well combined.

4. Pour grits mixture into prepared casserole. Bake until knife inserted in center comes out clean, about 45 minutes.

Each serving: About 338 calories, 16g protein, 24g carbohydrate, 21g total fat (12g saturated), 193mg cholesterol, 595mg sodium.

Portobello "Cheese Steaks"

Portobello "Cheese Steaks"

A hearty hand-held meal wrapped in pita and served gyro style.

PREP: 15 MINUTES   COOK: 20 MINUTES
MAKES 4 SANDWICHES.

2 medium portobello mushrooms
  (about 4 ounces each), stems
  removed
2 tablespoons olive oil
2 medium yellow peppers, thinly
  sliced
1 jumbo sweet onion (1 pound) such
  as Vidalia or Walla Walla, thinly
  sliced

$1/2$ teaspoon salt
$1/4$ teaspoon coarsely ground black
  pepper
2 tablespoons water
1 tablespoon balsamic vinegar
4 (7-inch) pocketless pitas
8 ounces part-skim mozzarella
  cheese, shredded (2 cups)

1. Preheat oven to 400°F. Heat nonstick 12-inch skillet over medium-high heat until hot. Brush both sides of mushrooms using 1 tablespoon oil. Add mushrooms to skillet and cook until tender and lightly browned, about 5 minutes on each side. Transfer mushrooms to cutting board and cut into $1/4$-inch-thick slices; set aside.

2. In same skillet, heat remaining 1 tablespoon oil over medium heat until hot. Add yellow peppers, onion, salt, black pepper, and water; cook, stirring frequently, until the vegetables are tender and golden, about 15 minutes. Stir in vinegar; remove skillet from heat. Gently stir in sliced portobellos.

3. Meanwhile, place pitas on large cookie sheet; sprinkle with mozzarella cheese. Heat pitas until cheese has melted, about 5 minutes.

4. Roll each pita into a cone; tightly wrap bottom half of each with kitchen parchment or foil to help hold its shape and prevent leakage. Fill pita cones with warm mushroom mixture.

Each sandwich: About 460 calories, 24g protein, 52g carbohydrate, 18g total fat (7g saturated), 41mg cholesterol, 1,060mg sodium.

Potato Pancakes and Carrot-Parsley Salad

There are as many recipes for potato pancakes as there are families that make them. To save time, we use a bag of preshredded hash-brown potatoes, which are found in the refrigerator case of your supermarket. To round out the meal, prepare the simple but tasty carrot salad.

PREP: 10 MINUTES   COOK: 15 MINUTES
MAKES 4 MAIN-DISH SERVINGS.

POTATO PANCAKES

1/2 cup vegetable oil for frying
1 teaspoon salt
1/8 teaspoon ground black pepper
2 large eggs
1 (20-ounce) bag refrigerated
   shredded hash-brown potatoes
   (4 cups)
2 green onions, trimmed and thinly
   sliced

CARROT-PARSLEY SALAD

1 tablespoon fresh lemon juice
1 tablespoon extravirgin olive oil
1/4 teaspoon salt
1 package (10 ounces) shredded
   carrots
1 cup packed fresh parsley leaves
applesauce and sour cream

1. Preheat oven to 250°F. Line the cookie sheet with paper towels. In 12-inch skillet, heat oil over medium–high heat until very hot.

2. Meanwhile, prepare pancakes: In medium bowl, mix salt, pepper, and eggs; stir in potatoes and green onions. Drop mixture by scant 1/2 cups into hot oil to make 4 pancakes. With back of spoon, flatten each pancake into 4-inch oval. Cook until golden on both sides, 5 to 7 minutes. With slotted spatula, transfer pancakes to prepared cookie sheet to drain; keep warm in oven. Repeat with remaining mixture.

3. While pancakes cook, prepare salad: In small bowl or cup, with fork, stir lemon juice, oil, and salt until blended.

4. In salad bowl, combine carrots and parsley. Pour dressing over salad and toss to coat evenly.

5. Serve pancakes with applesauce and sour cream, and a side of carrot-parsley salad.

Each serving: About 395 calories, 8g protein, 41g carbohydrate, 23g total fat (3g saturated), 106mg cholesterol, 890mg sodium.

Potato Pancakes and Carrot-Parsley Salad

French Potato Pancake

We've taken the classic Swiss shredded-potato pancake and come up with a choice of fillings designed to please everyone. This versatile recipe can serve as a main dish or an accompaniment.

PREP: 25 MINUTES BAKE: 25 MINUTES
MAKES 4 MAIN-DISH SERVINGS.

PEPPER FILLING
2 teaspoons olive oil
1 medium red pepper, cut into
  1/4-inch pieces
3 1/2 to 4 ounces plain goat cheese,
  crumbled

POTATO PANCAKE
2 1/4 pounds baking potatoes
  (about 4 medium)
1/2 teaspoon salt
1/2 teaspoon coarsely ground
  black pepper
2 tablespoons olive oil

1. Prepare filling: In oven-safe nonstick 10-inch skillet (if skillet is not oven-safe, wrap handle with double layer of foil), heat oil over medium heat until hot. Add red pepper and cook, stirring occasionally, until tender and lightly browned, 10 to 12 minutes. Transfer pepper to small bowl; set aside. Wipe skillet with paper towel.

2. Meanwhile, prepare potato pancake: Preheat oven to 400°F. Peel and coarsely shred potatoes; pat dry with paper towels. In large bowl, toss potatoes with salt and black pepper.

3. In same skillet, heat 1 tablespoon oil over medium heat. Working quickly, add half of potatoes, gently patting with rubber spatula to cover bottom of skillet. Leaving 1-inch border, top potatoes with red pepper and goat cheese. Cover filling with remaining potatoes, gently patting to edge of skillet. Cook, gently shaking skillet occasionally to keep pancake from sticking, until browned, 10 minutes.

4. Carefully invert pancake onto large, flat plate. Add remaining 1 tablespoon oil to skillet, then slide pancake back into skillet. Cook, gently shaking skillet occasionally, 10 minutes longer.

5. Place skillet, uncovered, in oven and bake until potatoes are tender throughout, 20 to 25 minutes.

Each serving: About 340 calories, 10g protein, 36g carbohydrate, 18g total fat (8g saturated), 22mg cholesterol, 550mg sodium.

French Potato Pancake

Swiss Potato Pancake: Prepare French Potato Pancake as above, but in step 1, instead of preparing pepper filling, heat *1 tablespoon oil* in skillet over medium heat until hot. Add *1 large onion (12 ounces)*, cut into 1/4-inch pieces, and cook, stirring occasionally, until tender and golden brown, about 15 minutes. Transfer onion to small bowl. Complete recipe as in steps 2 through 5, substituting caramelized onion and *1 cup shredded Gruyère cheese (4 ounces)* for red pepper and goat cheese.

Each serving: About 370 calories, 12g protein, 38g carbohydrate, 20g total fat (6g saturated), 30mg cholesterol, 380mg sodium.

Mexican Potato Pancake: Prepare French Potato Pancake as above, but in step 1, instead of preparing pepper filling, in small bowl, stir *1 cup canned black beans*, rinsed, drained, and mashed; *1 tablespoon water, 1 teaspoon fresh lime juice*, and *1/2 teaspoon ground cumin* until well mixed. (If bean mixture is too stiff to spread, stir in *1 or 2 teaspoons water*.) Complete recipe as in steps 2 through 5, substituting black-bean mixture and *1 cup shredded Monterey Jack cheese (4 ounces)* for red pepper and goat cheese.

Each serving: About 360 calories, 12g protein, 42g carbohydrate, 16g total fat (6g saturated), 30mg cholesterol, 530mg sodium.

Old-Time Tomato Sandwiches

We love these as is or with a few sprigs of watercress tucked inside.

PREP: 15 MINUTES
MAKES 4 SANDWICHES.

1 lemon
1/3 cup mayonnaise
1/4 teaspoon ground coriander
1/4 teaspoon salt
1/4 teaspoon coarsely ground black
  pepper

1 large round or oval loaf (1 pound)
  sourdough or other crusty bread
3 large ripe tomatoes, thickly sliced

1. From lemon, grate 1/2 teaspoon peel and squeeze 1 teaspoon juice. In small bowl, with fork, stir lemon peel and juice, mayonnaise, coriander, salt, and pepper until blended.

2. Cut eight 1/2-inch-thick slices from center of bread loaf. Reserve ends for another use. Toast bread if desired.

3. Spread 1 side of each bread slice with mayonnaise mixture. Top each of 4 bread slices, mayonnaise side up, with tomato slices; top with remaining bread slices, mayonnaise side down. Cut each sandwich in half to serve.

Each sandwich: About 300 calories, 6g protein, 35g carbohydrate, 18g total fat (3g saturated), 7mg cholesterol, 540mg sodium.

Old-Time Tomato Sandwiches

MAIN-DISH SALADS

Flatbread with Salad
recipe on page 82

Black Bean and Avocado Salad with Cilantro Dressing

A satisfying combination of summer veggies, romaine lettuce, and black beans tossed with a creamy cilantro-lime dressing.

PREP: 30 MINUTES

MAKES ABOUT 16 CUPS OR 4 MAIN-DISH SERVINGS.

CILANTRO DRESSING

2 limes
$1/4$ cup light mayonnaise
$1/2$ cup packed fresh cilantro leaves
2 tablespoons reduced-fat sour cream
$1/2$ teaspoon ground cumin
$1/4$ teaspoon sugar
$1/8$ teaspoon salt
$1/8$ teaspoon coarsely ground
    black pepper

SALAD

1 small head romaine lettuce (about 1 pound), cut into $3/4$-inch pieces (about 8 cups)
2 medium tomatoes, cut into $1/2$-inch pieces
2 Kirby cucumbers (about 4 ounces each), unpeeled, each cut lengthwise into quarters, then crosswise into $1/4$-inch-thick pieces
1 ripe avocado, cut into $1/2$-inch pieces
1 can (15 to 19 ounces) black beans, rinsed and drained

1. Prepare dressing: From limes, grate $1/2$ teaspoon peel and squeeze 3 tablespoons juice. In blender, combine lime peel and juice, mayonnaise, cilantro, sour cream, cumin, sugar, salt, and pepper and puree, occasionally scraping down sides of blender, until smooth. Cover and refrigerate if not using right away. Makes about $1/2$ cup.

2. Prepare salad: In large serving bowl, combine romaine, tomatoes, cucumbers, avocado, and beans. Add dressing and toss until evenly coated.

Each serving: About 230 calories, 9g protein, 34g carbohydrate, 10g total fat (2g saturated), 3mg cholesterol, 520mg sodium.

Wheat-Berry Salad with Spinach

Wheat berries, the whole unprocessed kernels, can be found in health food stores. They have a nutlike sweetness and a satisfyingly chewy texture.

PREP: 15 MINUTES PLUS SOAKING   COOK: 1 HOUR 15 MINUTES
MAKES 4 MAIN-DISH SERVINGS.

1 1/2 cups wheat berries (whole-grain wheat)
1 bunch (10 to 12 ounces) spinach, tough stems trimmed
1 medium tomato
10 dried tomato halves (about 1 ounce)
3 tablespoons olive oil

2 tablespoons red wine vinegar
1/2 teaspoon Dijon mustard
1 teaspoon salt
1/2 teaspoon sugar
1/4 teaspoon coarsely ground black pepper
1 cup golden raisins

1. In large bowl, soak wheat berries overnight in enough *water* to cover by 2 inches.

2. Drain wheat berries. In 4-quart saucepan, heat *7 cups water* to boiling over high heat. Add soaked wheat berries; heat to boiling. Reduce heat to low; cover and simmer until wheat berries are tender, about 1 hour. Drain.

3. Meanwhile, coarsely chop spinach. Chop tomato. Place dried tomato halves in small bowl; add *1 cup boiling water*. Let stand 5 minutes; drain well. Coarsely chop dried tomatoes.

4. Prepare dressing: In medium bowl, with wire whisk or fork, mix oil, vinegar, mustard, salt, sugar, and pepper until blended. Add raisins, diced tomato, chopped dried tomatoes, spinach, and wheat berries; toss well.

Each serving: About 455 calories, 12g protein, 82g carbohydrate, 12g total fat (1g saturated), 0mg cholesterol, 625mg sodium.

Penne with Green Beans and Basil

Penne with Green Beans and Basil

This cool pasta salad is perfect for a hot night.

PREP: 15 MINUTES   COOK: 20 MINUTES
MAKES 8 CUPS OR 4 MAIN-DISH SERVINGS.

8 ounces penne or bow-tie pasta
1 pound green beans, trimmed and
   each cut in half
1 1/2 teaspoons salt
1 tablespoon water
1 cup loosely packed fresh
   basil leaves

1/4 cup extravirgin olive oil
1/2 teaspoon coarsely ground
   black pepper
1 medium tomato, chopped
small basil leaves for garnish

1. In large saucepot, cook penne as label directs.

2. Meanwhile, in 12-inch skillet, heat *1 inch water* to boiling over high heat. Add green beans and 1/2 teaspoon salt; heat to boiling. Cook beans until tender-crisp, 8 to 10 minutes. Drain beans. Rinse beans under cold running water to cool slightly; drain again.

3. In blender at high speed, combine basil, oil, and water and puree until almost smooth, stopping blender occasionally and scraping down sides with rubber spatula. Transfer basil puree to large bowl; stir in remaining 1 teaspoon salt and pepper.

4. Drain pasta; rinse under cold running water and drain again. In warm serving bowl, toss pasta, beans, tomato, and basil puree. Garnish with basil leaves.

Each serving: About 370 calories, 10g protein, 52g carbohydrate, 15g total fat (2g saturated), 0mg cholesterol, 680mg sodium.

Rice Noodles with Many Herbs

Whip up this light summer main dish with fast-cooking noodles, carrots, cucumber, herbs, and our delicious Asian dressing. Serve warm or at room temperature.

PREP: 20 MINUTES   COOK: 10 MINUTES
MAKES 4 MAIN-DISH SERVINGS.

3 small carrots, peeled and cut into 2" by 1/4" matchstick strips (1 1/3 cups)

1/3 cup seasoned rice vinegar

1 package (1 pound) 1/2-inch-wide flat rice noodles

1/3 English (seedless) cucumber, unpeeled and cut into 2" by 1/4" matchstick strips (1 cup)

1 cup loosely packed fresh cilantro leaves

1/2 cup loosely packed fresh mint leaves

1/3 cup loosely packed small fresh basil leaves

1/3 cup snipped fresh chives

2 teaspoons Asian sesame oil

1. In small bowl, stir carrots with rice vinegar. Let stand at room temperature while preparing noodles.

2. In 8-quart saucepot, heat *5 quarts water* to boiling over high heat. Add noodles and cook just until cooked through, about 3 minutes. Drain noodles; rinse under cold running water and drain again.

3. Transfer noodles to large shallow serving bowl. Add carrots with their liquid, cucumber, cilantro, mint, basil, chives, and sesame oil; toss well.

Each serving: About 470 calories, 7g protein, 105g carbohydrate, 3g total fat (0g saturated), 0mg cholesterol, 550mg sodium.

Rice Noodles with Many Herbs

Tomato and Orzo Salad

This perfect pasta toss requires little cooking but yields big flavor.

PREP: 20 MINUTES   COOK: 8 MINUTES
MAKES ABOUT 7 1/2 CUPS OR 4 MAIN-DISH SERVINGS.

salt
1¼ cups orzo pasta
½ pound green beans, trimmed and each cut into thirds
2 large lemons
2 tablespoons extravirgin olive oil
2 teaspoons fresh oregano leaves, chopped

¼ teaspoon coarsely ground black pepper
1 pound ripe tomatoes (about 3 medium), cut into ½-inch pieces
4 ounces ricotta salata cheese, crumbled, or Parmesan cheese, shaved

1. In 4-quart saucepan, heat *3 quarts of salted water* to boiling over high heat. Add orzo; heat to boiling and cook 4 minutes. Add green beans and cook until orzo and beans are tender, about 4 minutes longer. Drain well.
2. Meanwhile, from lemons, grate 1 teaspoon peel and squeeze ¼ cup juice. In large bowl, with wire whisk or fork, mix oil, oregano, 3/4 teaspoon salt, pepper, and lemon peel and juice until blended.
3. Add warm orzo and beans to dressing in bowl and toss well. Gently stir in tomatoes and ricotta salata.

Each serving: About 340 calories, 12g protein, 44g carbohydrate, 14g total fat (6g saturated), 26mg cholesterol, 1,010mg sodium.

Fattoush

This Lebanese salad is packed with juicy summer-ripe tomatoes and fresh herbs. Pieces of toasted pita absorb the tasty dressing.

PREP: 25 MINUTES PLUS STANDING
MAKES ABOUT 16 CUPS OR 4 MAIN-DISH SERVINGS.

3 tablespoons fresh lemon juice
3 tablespoons olive oil
1 teaspoon salt
1/2 teaspoon coarsely ground
   black pepper
4 medium tomatoes (about 1 1/4
   pounds), cut into 1/2-inch pieces
3 green onions, trimmed and chopped
1 medium cucumber (8 ounces),
   peeled, seeded, and cut into
   1/2-inch pieces

1 cup loosely packed fresh
   parsley leaves
1/2 cup loosely packed fresh
   mint leaves, chopped
4 (6-inch) pitas, each split
   horizontally in half
1 small head romaine lettuce (about
   1 pound), coarsely chopped

1. In large salad bowl, with wire whisk or fork, mix lemon juice, oil, salt, and pepper. Add tomatoes, green onions, cucumber, parsley, and mint; toss to coat. Let tomato mixture stand 15 minutes to allow flavors to blend.

2. Meanwhile, toast pitas; cool. Break pitas into 1-inch pieces.

3. Just before serving, toss lettuce and pitas with tomato mixture.

Each serving: About 315 calories, 9g protein, 47g carbohydrate, 12g total fat (2g saturated), 0mg cholesterol, 935mg sodium.

Greek Pasta Toss

Greek Pasta Toss

A great Greek salad (minus the lettuce) with hot pasta and beans folded in makes a complete meal.

PREP: 25 MINUTES   COOK: 15 MINUTES
MAKES 6 MAIN-DISH SERVINGS.

1 pound rotini or fusilli pasta
1/4 cup olive oil
2 tablespoons balsamic vinegar
1 garlic clove, crushed with garlic press
1/2 teaspoon salt
1/4 teaspoon coarsely ground black pepper
9 ripe medium tomatoes (about 3 pounds), cut into thin wedges
2 cans (15 to 19 ounces each) garbanzo beans, rinsed and drained

8 ounces feta cheese, coarsely crumbled
2 Kirby cucumbers (about 4 ounces each), unpeeled and cut into 1/4-inch pieces
1/2 cup Kalamata olives, pitted and chopped
1/2 cup packed fresh parsley leaves, chopped
1/2 cup packed fresh dill, chopped

1. In large saucepot, cook pasta as label directs.
2. Meanwhile, in large serving bowl, with wire whisk, mix oil, vinegar, garlic, salt, and pepper until blended. Add tomatoes, beans, feta, cucumbers, olives, parsley, and dill. Toss until evenly mixed and coated with dressing.
3. Drain pasta. Add pasta to tomato mixture in bowl; toss well.

Each serving: About 685 calories, 26g protein, 97g carbohydrate, 22g total fat (8g saturated), 34mg cholesterol, 1,154mg sodium.

Greek Peasant Salad

Serve this cool Mediterranean-style on a summer night.

PREP: 25 MINUTES
MAKES ABOUT 6 1/2 CUPS OR 4 MAIN-DISH SERVINGS.

4 Kirby cucumbers (about 1 pound)
2 tablespoons fresh lemon juice
1 tablespoon olive oil
1/4 teaspoon salt
1/8 teaspoon ground black pepper
2 pounds ripe red and/or yellow
   tomatoes (about 6 medium), cut
   into 1-inch pieces

1/2 cup loosely packed fresh mint
   leaves, chopped
1/3 cup Kalamata olives, pitted and
   coarsely chopped
1/4 cup loosely packed fresh dill,
   chopped
2 ounces feta cheese, crumbled
   (1/2 cup)

1. With vegetable peeler, remove 3 or 4 evenly spaced lengthwise strips of peel from each cucumber. Cut each cucumber lengthwise into quarters, then crosswise into 1/2-inch pieces.

2. In large bowl, with wire whisk or fork, mix lemon juice, oil, salt, and pepper until blended. Add cucumbers, tomatoes, mint, olives, and dill, and toss until evenly mixed and coated with dressing. Top with feta.

Each serving: About 150 calories, 5g protein, 17g carbohydrate, 9g total fat (3g saturated), 12mg cholesterol, 42g sodium.

Greek Peasant Salad

Flatbread with Salad

Try this salad "pizza" as an alternative to the usual tomato-and-cheese kind. It's especially good because it starts with our excellent crusty Grilled Flatbread.

Prep: 20 minutes plus preparation of flatbreads
Makes 4 main-dish servings.

GRILLED FLATBREAD
1 package active dry yeast
1 teaspoon sugar
1¼ cups warm water (105°F to 115°F)
about 4 cups all-purpose flour
about 3 tablespoons olive oil
2 teaspoons salt

SALAD
2 tablespoons extravirgin olive oil
2 tablespoons red wine vinegar

1 teaspoon sugar
1 teaspoon Dijon mustard
¼ teaspoon salt
⅛ teaspoon ground black pepper
6 cups salad greens, such as radicchio, endive, and arugula, torn into ½-inch pieces
2 ripe medium tomatoes, cut into ½-inch pieces
1 small cucumber, peeled and cut into ½-inch pieces

1. Prepare flatbread: In large bowl, combine yeast, sugar, and ¼ cup warm water; stir to dissolve. Let stand until foamy, about 5 minutes. With a wooden spoon, stir in 1½ cups flour, 2 tablespoons olive oil, salt, and remaining 1 cup warm water until blended. With spoon, gradually stir in 2 cups flour. With floured hand, knead mixture in bowl to combine.

2. Turn dough onto lightly floured surface and knead, working in more flour (about ½ cup), until smooth and elastic, about 10 minutes.

3. Shape dough into ball and place in greased large bowl, turning to grease top. Cover bowl with plastic wrap and let rise in warm place (80°F to 85°F) until doubled in volume, about 1 hour. (After dough has risen, if not using dough right away, punch down and leave in bowl, cover loosely with greased plastic wrap, and refrigerate until ready to use, up to 24 hours. When ready to use, follow directions below.)

4. Punch down dough. Turn dough onto lightly floured surface. Cover and let rest 15 minutes.

5. Meanwhile, prepare grill. Grease two large cookie sheets.

6. Shape dough into 4 balls. On lightly floured surface, with floured rolling pin, roll 1 dough ball at a time into 12-inch round about ⅛ inch thick. (The diameter or shape of round is not as important as even thick-

Flatbread with Salad

ness.) Place rounds on prepared cookie sheets; lightly brush tops with some remaining oil.

7. About 10 minutes before grilling flatbread, prepare salad topping: In large bowl, with wire whisk, mix oil, vinegar, sugar, mustard, salt, and pepper until blended. Add salad greens, tomatoes, and cucumber; toss to coat well. Set aside.

8. With hands, place 1 round at a time, greased side down, on hot grill rack over medium heat. Grill until grill marks appear on underside and dough stiffens (dough may puff slightly), 2 to 3 minutes. Brush top with some oil. With tongs, turn bread and grill until grill marks appear on underside and bread is cooked through, 2 to 3 minutes longer. Transfer flatbread to tray; keep warm. Repeat with remaining dough rounds.

9. To serve, top each flatbread with about 2 cups salad. Cut each round into quarters. Serve 4 wedges per person.

Each serving of flatbread: About 370 calories, 10g protein, 64g carbohydrate, 8g total fat (2g saturated), 0mg cholesterol, 610mg sodium.

Each serving of flatbread with salad: About 620 calories, 16g protein, 106g carbohydrate, 14g total fat (2g saturated), 0mg cholesterol, 1,250mg sodium.

Szechuan Peanut-Noodle Salad

A tasty pasta salad packed with great Asian flavors. To serve cold, chill the pasta and toss with the vegetables just before serving.

PREP: 25 MINUTES   COOK: 25 MINUTES
MAKES 5 MAIN-DISH SERVINGS.

1 package (16 ounces) linguine or
  spaghetti
2 1/2 teaspoons salt
4 ounces snow peas, strings removed
1/2 cup creamy peanut butter
1 tablespoon grated, peeled
  fresh ginger
1/4 cup soy sauce

2 tablespoons distilled white vinegar
2 teaspoons Asian sesame oil
1/4 teaspoon hot pepper sauce
1 small cucumber (6 ounces), peeled,
  seeded, and cut into 2" by 1/4"
  matchstick strips
1/4 cup dry-roasted peanuts
1 green onion, trimmed and chopped

1. In large saucepot, cook linguine as label directs, using 2 teaspoons salt.

2. Meanwhile, in 3-quart saucepan, heat *1 inch water* to boiling; add snow peas. Reduce heat and simmer 2 minutes; drain. Rinse with cold running water; drain. Cut snow peas lengthwise into 1/4-inch-wide matchstick strips; set aside.

3. Drain linguine, reserving 1 cup pasta water.

4. Prepare dressing: In large bowl, with wire whisk, mix peanut butter, ginger, reserved pasta water, soy sauce, vinegar, sesame oil, hot pepper sauce, and remaining 1/2 teaspoon salt until smooth.

5. Add linguine to dressing in bowl and toss to coat. Add snow peas and cucumber; toss to combine. Sprinkle with peanuts and green onion.

Each serving: About 572 calories, 22g protein, 78g carbohydrate, 20g total fat (3g saturated), 0mg cholesterol, 1,794mg sodium.

Egg Salad Deluxe

Hard-cooked eggs are chopped and mixed with sautéed onions, mushrooms, and celery for a new take on the classic egg salad. If you like, serve with toasted whole-grain bread.

PREP: 20 MINUTES   COOK: 20 MINUTES
MAKES ABOUT 4 1/2 CUPS OR 6 MAIN-DISH SERVINGS.

8 large eggs
3 tablespoons olive oil
1 medium onion, cut in half and thinly sliced
10 ounces mushrooms, sliced
2 medium stalks celery, finely chopped
1/4 cup loosely packed fresh parsley leaves, chopped
1/2 teaspoon salt
1/4 teaspoon coarsely ground black pepper
1 head Boston lettuce, leaves separated

1. In 3-quart saucepan, place eggs and enough *cold water* to cover by at least 1 inch; heat to boiling over high heat. Immediately remove saucepan from heat and cover tightly; let stand 15 minutes. Pour off hot water and run cold water over eggs until easy to handle.

2. Meanwhile, in nonstick 12-inch skillet, heat 1 tablespoon oil over medium heat until hot. Add onion and cook, stirring occasionally, until tender and golden, 10 to 12 minutes. Increase heat to medium-high; add mushrooms and cook until mushrooms are golden and all liquid has evaporated, about 8 minutes.

3. Peel hard-cooked eggs and finely chop. In large bowl, combine eggs with mushroom mixture, celery, parsley, salt, pepper, and remaining 2 tablespoons oil; toss well.

4. To serve, line platter with lettuce leaves and top with egg salad.

Each serving: About 190 calories, 11g protein, 5g carbohydrate, 14g total fat (3g saturated), 283mg cholesterol, 290mg sodium.

QUICK
DINNERS

Spinach Soufflé
recipe on page 102

Southwestern Black Bean Burgers

For a second easy weeknight meal, make a double batch and freeze the uncooked burgers. Defrost 10 minutes, then cook, turning once, until heated through, about 12 minutes.

PREP: 10 MINUTES   COOK: 6 MINUTES
MAKES 4 SANDWICHES.

1 can (15 to 19 ounces) black beans, rinsed and drained
2 tablespoons light mayonnaise
1/4 cup packed fresh cilantro leaves, chopped
1 tablespoon plain dried bread crumbs
1/2 teaspoon ground cumin
1/2 teaspoon hot pepper sauce
nonstick cooking spray
1 cup loosely packed sliced lettuce
4 mini (4-inch) whole-wheat pitas, warmed
1/2 cup mild salsa

1. In large bowl, with potato masher or fork, mash beans with mayonnaise until almost smooth with some lumps. Stir in cilantro, bread crumbs, cumin, and pepper sauce until combined. With lightly floured hands, shape bean mixture into four 3-inch round patties. Spray both sides of each patty lightly with nonstick cooking spray.

2. Heat 10-inch skillet over medium heat until hot. Add patties and cook until lightly browned, about 3 minutes. With pancake turner, turn patties over, and cook until heated through, 3 minutes longer.

3. Arrange lettuce on pitas; top with burgers then salsa.

Each sandwich: About 210 calories, 13g protein, 42g carbohydrate, 3g total fat (0g saturated), 0mg cholesterol, 715mg sodium.

Southwestern Black Bean Burgers

Couscous with Garbanzo Beans

Couscous with Garbanzo Beans

A vegetarian entrée fragrant with the flavors of Morocco—warm spices, green olives, and garlic—gets a quick start from preseasoned couscous mix.

PREP: 5 MINUTES   COOK: 10 MINUTES
MAKES 4 MAIN-DISH SERVINGS.

1 box (5.6 ounces) couscous (Moroccan pasta) with toasted pine nuts
1/3 cup dark seedless raisins
1 tablespoon olive oil
1 medium zucchini (about 10 ounces), cut lengthwise in half, then crosswise into 1/2-inch-thick slices
1 garlic clove, crushed with garlic press

3/4 teaspoon ground cumin
3/4 teaspoon ground coriander
1/8 teaspoon ground red pepper (cayenne)
2 cans (15 to 19 ounces each) garbanzo beans, rinsed and drained
1/2 cup salad olives, drained, or chopped pimiento-stuffed olives
1/4 cup water

1. Prepare couscous as label directs, except add raisins to cooking water.
2. Meanwhile, in nonstick 12-inch skillet, heat oil over medium-high heat until hot. Add zucchini and cook, stirring occasionally, 5 minutes. Add garlic, cumin, coriander, and red pepper and cook, stirring, 30 seconds. Add beans, olives, and water and cook, stirring often, until heated through, about 5 minutes.
3. Add cooked couscous to bean mixture and toss gently. Spoon into serving bowl.

Each serving: About 555 calories, 20g protein, 101g carbohydrate, 10g total fat (1g saturated), 0mg cholesterol, 1,110mg sodium.

Fast Fried Rice

The secrets to this dish are quick-cooking brown rice, precut frozen vegetables, and ready-to-use stir-fry sauce.

PREP: 5 MINUTES COOK: 15 MINUTES
MAKES 4 MAIN-DISH SERVINGS.

1½ cups quick-cooking brown rice
1 pound firm tofu, drained and cut
  into 1-inch cubes
6 teaspoons olive oil
1 package (16 ounces) frozen
  vegetables for stir-fry

2 large eggs, lightly beaten
⅓ cup stir-fry sauce
¼ cup water

1. Prepare rice as label directs.

2. Meanwhile, in medium bowl, place 3 layers paper towels. Place tofu on towels and top with 3 more layers paper towels. With hand, gently press tofu to extract excess moisture.

3. In nonstick 12-inch skillet, heat 2 teaspoons oil over medium-high heat until hot. Add frozen vegetables; cover and cook, stirring occasionally, 5 minutes. Transfer vegetables to bowl; keep warm.

4. In same skillet, heat remaining 4 teaspoons oil until hot. Add tofu and cook, stirring gently, 5 minutes. Stir in cooked rice and cook 4 minutes longer.

5. With spatula, push rice mixture around edge of skillet, leaving space in center. Add eggs to center of skillet; cook, stirring eggs until scrambled, about 1 minute. Add stir-fry sauce, vegetables, and water; cook, stirring, 1 minute.

Each serving: About 360 calories, 17g protein, 41g carbohydrate, 15g total fat (2g saturated), 106mg cholesterol, 760mg sodium.

Fast Fried Rice

Fusilli with Garbanzo Beans and Spinach

Fusilli with Garbanzo Beans and Spinach

A staple of Italian cuisine, beans show up almost everywhere, including pasta dishes. For this dish, we use canned garbanzo beans to reduce preparation and cooking time.

PREP: 8 MINUTES   COOK: 12 MINUTES
MAKES 6 MAIN-DISH SERVINGS.

1 pound fusilli pasta
2 tablespoons olive oil
1 medium onion, chopped
2 garlic cloves, crushed with garlic press
1/2 teaspoon dried oregano
1 can (29 ounces) garbanzo beans,

rinsed and drained
3 tablespoons balsamic vinegar
1 1/4 teaspoons salt
1/4 teaspoon coarsely ground black pepper
2 bags (6 ounces each) baby spinach

1. In large saucepot, cook pasta as label directs.
2. Meanwhile, in 12-inch skillet, heat oil over medium-high heat until hot. Add onion; cook, covered, 5 minutes, stirring often. Stir in garlic and oregano and cook 30 seconds. Stir in beans, vinegar, salt, and pepper; cook, stirring often, 5 minutes.
3. Drain pasta, reserving 1 cup pasta water. Return pasta to saucepot. Add spinach, bean mixture, and reserved pasta water; toss gently to combine.

Each serving: About 500 calories, 20g protein, 85g carbohydrate, 8g total fat (1g saturated), 0mg cholesterol, 980mg sodium.

Cavatelli with Ricotta and Fresh Tomato Sauce

We used frozen cavatelli—a short, curled, rippled pasta. If you can't find it, substitute frozen gnocchi. Serve with mixed Italian salad greens and sesame breadsticks. Just before serving, toss the greens with olive oil and a squeeze of lemon juice.

PREP: 5 MINUTES COOK: 25 MINUTES
MAKES 4 MAIN-DISH SERVINGS.

1 bag (16 ounces) frozen cavatelli
1 tablespoon olive oil
1 garlic clove, crushed with garlic press
4 medium tomatoes (about 1 1/2 pounds), chopped

1/2 teaspoon salt
1/4 teaspoon coarsely ground black pepper
3/4 cup part-skim ricotta cheese
1/4 cup freshly grated Pecorino Romano or Parmesan cheese

1. In large saucepot, cook pasta as label directs.
2. Meanwhile, in nonstick 10-inch skillet, heat oil over medium heat until hot. Add garlic and cook, stirring, 1 minute. Stir in tomatoes, salt, and pepper and cook, stirring occasionally, until tomatoes break up slightly, about 5 minutes.
3. Drain cavatelli; transfer to warm serving bowl. Stir in ricotta and Romano. Pour tomato mixture on top; toss before serving.

Each serving: About 455 calories, 20g protein, 71g carbohydrate, 11g total fat (5g saturated), 40mg cholesterol, 560mg sodium.

Fettuccine with Creamy Tomato Sauce and Peas

Quick-cooking fresh pasta is tossed with chunky tomato sauce simmered with heavy cream.

PREP: 5 MINUTES   COOK: 15 MINUTES
MAKES 4 MAIN-DISH SERVINGS.

2 packages (9 ounces each) fresh (refrigerated) fettuccine
1 can (14 1/2 ounces) seasoned chunky tomatoes for pasta
1 can (15 ounces) tomato sauce
1/3 cup heavy or whipping cream
1 package (10 ounces) frozen peas
freshly grated Parmesan cheese (optional)

1. In large saucepot, cook pasta as label directs.
2. Meanwhile, in 2-quart saucepan, heat tomatoes, tomato sauce, and cream to boiling over medium-high heat. Reduce heat to medium and cook, stirring, 2 minutes.
3. Place frozen peas in colander. Drain fettuccine over peas. In large warm serving bowl, toss fettuccine and peas with tomato mixture. Serve with Parmesan, if you like.

Each serving: About 575 calories, 22g protein, 96g carbohydrate, 13g total fat (6g saturated), 158mg cholesterol, 1,375mg sodium.

Pasta Ribbons with Chunky Vegtables

Pasta Ribbons with Chunky Vegetables

Just as satisfying as lasagna but with half the work and half the time.

PREP: 10 MINUTES   COOK: 15 MINUTES
MAKES 4 MAIN-DISH SERVINGS.

salt

1 package (8 to 9 ounces) oven-ready lasagna noodles (6½" by 3½" each)

1 tablespoon olive oil

2 medium yellow summer squash and/or zucchini (10 ounces each), cut into ¾-inch-thick slices

1 package (10 ounces) mushrooms, trimmed and cut into halves or quarters, if large

2 cups tomato-basil pasta sauce

¼ cup heavy or whipping cream

1 small chunk (2 ounces) Parmesan cheese

1. In 4-quart saucepan, heat 3 quarts of *salted water* to boiling over high heat. Add lasagna noodles, 1 noodle at a time to avoid sticking; cook until tender, 7 to 8 minutes.

2. Meanwhile, in nonstick 12-inch skillet, heat oil over medium-high heat until very hot. Add squash and mushrooms; cover and cook, stirring occasionally, until vegetables are tender-crisp, 4 to 5 minutes. Add pasta sauce and cream; heat to boiling, stirring frequently.

3. Drain noodles. In serving bowl, toss noodles with squash mixture. With vegetable peeler, shave thin strips from Parmesan. Top pasta with Parmesan shavings to serve.

Each serving: About 515 calories, 19g protein, 70g carbohydrate, 18g total fat (7g saturated), 32mg cholesterol, 770mg sodium.

Poblano Rigatoni

Poblano Rigatoni

No need to fire up the grill. You'll get the same char-roasted flavor by searing the poblanos in a hot skillet—and you won't have to peel the chiles either!

PREP: 10 MINUTES COOK: 20 MINUTES
MAKES 4 MAIN-DISH SERVINGS.

1 package (16 ounces) rigatoni pasta
1 tablespoon olive oil
3 poblano chiles (8 ounces) or 2 large green peppers, cut into 1/2-inch strips
1 small onion, cut into 1/2-inch-thick slices
2 small zucchini (about 6 ounces each), cut into 1/2-inch-thick slices
2 garlic cloves, crushed with garlic press
1/2 teaspoon dried oregano, crumbled
1 teaspoon salt
1 pint grape or cherry tomatoes
4 ounces Monterey Jack cheese, cut into 1/2-inch pieces

1. In large saucepot, cook pasta as label directs.
2. Meanwhile, in nonstick 12-inch skillet, heat oil over medium-high heat until hot. Add chiles and onion; cook until lightly charred and tender-crisp, about 7 minutes. Add zucchini; cover and cook 3 minutes. Add garlic, oregano, and salt; cook 30 seconds. Stir in tomatoes; cover and cook until slightly softened.
3. Drain pasta. In serving bowl, toss pasta with vegetables and cheese.

Each serving: About 635 calories, 25g protein, 100g carbohydrate, 15g total fat (7g saturated), 30mg cholesterol, 925mg sodium.

Spinach Soufflé

Even though this recipe requires about 40 minutes total, only 20 minutes are active prep. During the remaining 20 minutes, while the soufflé bakes, you can relax! Serve with crusty rolls and a salad of mixed baby greens.

PREP: 20 MINUTES   BAKE: 20 MINUTES

MAKES 4 MAIN-DISH SERVINGS.

3 tablespoons plain dried bread crumbs
1¹/₂ cups low-fat milk (1%)
¹/₃ cup cornstarch
2 large eggs, separated
1 package (10 ounces) frozen chopped spinach, thawed and squeezed dry

3 tablespoons freshly grated Parmesan cheese
¹/₂ teaspoon salt
¹/₄ teaspoon coarsely ground black pepper
¹/₂ teaspoon cream of tartar
4 large egg whites (see Tip below)

1. Preheat oven to 425°F. Spray 10-inch quiche dish or shallow 2-quart casserole with nonstick cooking spray; sprinkle with bread crumbs to coat. Set aside.

2. In 2-quart saucepan, with wire whisk, beat milk with cornstarch until blended. Heat milk mixture over medium-high heat, stirring constantly, until mixture thickens and boils; boil 1 minute. Remove pan from heat.

3. In large bowl, with rubber spatula, mix egg yolks, spinach, Parmesan, salt, and pepper until blended; stir in warm milk mixture. Cool slightly (if spinach mixture is too warm, it will deflate beaten egg whites).

4. In another large bowl, with mixer at high speed, beat cream of tartar and 6 egg whites until stiff peaks form. Gently fold egg-white mixture, one-third at a time, into spinach mixture.

5. Spoon soufflé mixture into quiche dish. Bake soufflé until top is golden and puffed, about 20 minutes. Serve immediately.

Each serving: About 195 calories, 15g protein, 23g carbohydrate, 5g total fat (2g saturated), 114mg cholesterol, 590mg sodium.

Tip

If you prefer, you can use liquid egg substitute or pasteurized liquid egg whites, which are sold in 1-pint containers in the dairy case of most supermarkets.

Spinach Soufflé

Herb and Feta Frittata

Packed with fresh herbs, this frittata is guaranteed to wake up any palate. Feel free to experiment by using your favorite fresh herbs: oregano, marjoram, or chervil to name just a few.

PREP: 15 MINUTES   BAKE: 15 MINUTES
MAKES 4 MAIN-DISH SERVINGS.

2 teaspoons olive oil
8 large eggs
4 ounces feta cheese, crumbled
1/3 cup loosely packed fresh parsley
  or basil leaves, chopped

1/4 cup whole milk
2 tablespoons fresh rosemary or
  thyme leaves, chopped
1/2 teaspoon ground black pepper

1. Preheat oven to 400°F. In oven-safe nonstick 10-inch skillet (if skillet is not oven-safe, wrap handle with double layer of foil), heat oil over medium heat until hot.

2. Meanwhile, in medium bowl, with wire whisk, beat eggs, feta, parsley, milk, rosemary, and pepper until blended. Pour egg mixture into skillet; do not stir. Cook until egg mixture begins to set around edge, 3 to 4 minutes.

3. Place skillet in oven; bake until frittata is set, 13 to 15 minutes. Cut frittata into wedges to serve.

Each serving: About 255 calories, 17g protein, 4g carbohydrate, 19g total fat (8g saturated), 452mg cholesterol, 450mg sodium.

Herb and Feta Frittata

Nacho Casserole

Warning: This soup-based casserole may become a family favorite! For less "heat," omit the jalapeños.

PREP: 10 MINUTES   BAKE: 20 MINUTES
MAKES 6 MAIN-DISH SERVINGS.

1 can (10³/₄ ounces) condensed Cheddar cheese soup

¹/₂ cup low-fat milk (1%)

1 jar (16 ounces) mild or medium-hot salsa

1 bag (7 ounces) baked, unsalted tortilla chips

1 can (16 ounces) fat-free refried beans

1 or 2 jalapeño chiles, thinly sliced

1 cup shredded Cheddar cheese

Preheat oven to 400°F. In 13" by 9" ceramic or glass baking dish, stir undiluted soup with milk until well blended; spread evenly. Top with half of salsa and half of chips. Carefully spread beans over chips. Top with remaining chips and salsa. Sprinkle evenly with chiles and Cheddar. Bake until hot, about 20 minutes.

Each serving: About 385 calories, 17g protein, 60g carbohydrate, 12g total fat (5g saturated), 27mg cholesterol, 1,370mg sodium.

Nacho Casserole

Mexican Potato Frittata

This flat, baked omelet combines a jar of salsa with a bit of sharp Cheddar cheese. Toss a package of prewashed baby spinach with sliced red onions, sliced fresh pears, and bottled salad dressing while the frittata bakes.

PREP: 20 MINUTES   BAKE: 5 MINUTES
MAKES 4 MAIN-DISH SERVINGS.

1 teaspoon olive oil
12 ounces red-skinned potatoes, cut into 1/2-inch pieces
6 large eggs
1 jar (11 to 12 ounces) medium-hot salsa

1/2 teaspoon salt
1/4 teaspoon coarsely ground black pepper
1/4 cup shredded sharp Cheddar cheese (1 ounce)
1 medium tomato

1. Preheat oven to 425°F. In oven-safe nonstick 10-inch skillet (if skillet is not oven-safe, wrap handle with double layer of foil), heat oil over medium-high heat until hot; add potatoes and cook, covered, until potatoes are tender and golden brown, about 10 minutes, stirring occasionally.

2. Meanwhile, in medium bowl, with wire whisk or fork, beat eggs with 1/4 cup salsa (chopped, if necessary), salt, and pepper. Stir in cheese; set aside. Chop tomato and stir into remaining salsa.

3. Stir egg mixture into potatoes in skillet and cook over medium heat, covered, until egg mixture begins to set around edge, about 3 minutes. Remove cover and place skillet in oven; bake until frittata is set, 4 to 6 minutes.

4. To serve, transfer frittata to cutting board. Cut into wedges and top with salsa mixture.

Each serving: About 235 calories, 14g protein, 20g carbohydrate, 11g total fat (4g saturated), 327mg cholesterol, 795mg sodium.

Tofu Stir-fry

We call for a bag of broccoli flowerets to save cutting and trimming time. Choose extrafirm tofu; other types will fall apart during stir-frying. To serve, spoon the saucy mixture over quick-cooking brown rice, another time-saver.

PREP: 25 MINUTES   COOK: 15 MINUTES
MAKES 4 MAIN-DISH SERVINGS.

3 tablespoons soy sauce
1 tablespoon brown sugar
1 tablespoon cornstarch
1 cup water
2 teaspoons vegetable oil
3 garlic cloves, crushed with garlic press
1 tablespoon peeled, grated fresh ginger
1/8 to 1/4 teaspoon crushed red pepper

1 bag (12 ounces) broccoli flowerets, cut into uniform pieces if necessary
8 ounces shiitake mushrooms, stems removed and caps thinly sliced
1 medium red pepper, cut into 1-inch pieces
1 package (15 ounces) extafirm tofu, patted dry and cut into 1-inch cubes
3 green onions, trimmed and thinly sliced

1. In small bowl, with wire whisk, mix soy sauce, brown sugar, corn-starch, and water until blended; set aside.

2. In deep nonstick 12-inch skillet, heat oil over medium-high heat until hot. Add garlic, ginger, and crushed red pepper and cook, stirring frequently (stir-frying), 30 seconds. Add broccoli, mushrooms, and red pepper and cook, covered, 8 minutes, stirring occasionally.

3. Add tofu and green onions and cook, uncovered, 2 minutes, stirring occasionally. Stir soy-sauce mixture to blend and add to skillet; heat to boiling. Boil, stirring, 1 minute.

Each serving: About 225 calories, 16g protein, 23g carbohydrate, 9g total fat (1g saturated), 0mg cholesterol, 775mg sodium.

Tofu Stir-fry

Ricotta-Spinach Calzone

Using refrigerated pizza-crust dough simplifies and shortens the preparation of these rich cheese and spinach–filled "pies."

PREP: 10 MINUTES   BAKE: 25 MINUTES
MAKES 4 MAIN-DISH SERVINGS.

1 cup part-skim ricotta cheese
1 cup shredded mozzarella cheese (4 ounces)
1 tablespoon cornstarch
1/2 teaspoon dried oregano
1 tube (10 ounces) refrigerated pizza-crust dough

1/2 cup marinara sauce
1 package (10 ounces) frozen chopped spinach, thawed and squeezed dry

1. Preheat oven to 400°F. In small bowl, combine ricotta, mozzarella, cornstarch, and oregano; stir until blended. Set aside.

2. Spray large cookie sheet with nonstick cooking spray. Unroll pizza dough in center of cookie sheet. With fingertips, press dough into 14" by 10" rectangle.

3. Spread cheese mixture lengthwise on half of dough, leaving 1-inch border. Spoon marinara sauce over cheese mixture; top with spinach. Fold other half of dough over filling. Pinch edges together to seal.

4. Bake calzone until well browned on top, 20 to 25 minutes. Cut calzone into 4 equal pieces to serve.

Each serving: About 400 calories, 21g protein, 43g carbohydrate, 15g total fat (5g saturated), 19mg cholesterol, 1,055mg sodium.

Skillet Vegetable Curry

A package of precut cauliflower shortens prep time. As vegetables simmer, toast pita bread.

PREP: 15 MINUTES   COOK: 25 MINUTES
MAKES ABOUT 8 CUPS OR 4 MAIN-DISH SERVINGS.

3/4 pound cauliflower flowerets
1 large all-purpose potato (about
    8 ounces), peeled and cut into
    1-inch pieces
1 large sweet potato (about
    12 ounces), peeled and cut into
    1-inch pieces
2 tablespoons lightly packed
    sweetened flaked coconut
2 teaspoons olive oil
1 medium onion, finely chopped

1 teaspoon mustard seeds
1 1/2 teaspoons ground cumin
1 1/2 teaspoons ground coriander
1/8 teaspoon ground red pepper
    (cayenne)
2 medium tomatoes, chopped
1 cup frozen peas, thawed
1 1/4 teaspoons salt
1/2 cup loosely packed fresh
    cilantro leaves, chopped

1. In 4-quart saucepan, combine cauliflower, potato, sweet potato, and enough *water* to cover; heat to boiling over high heat. Reduce heat to low; cover and simmer until vegetables are tender, 8 to 10 minutes. Drain well, reserving 3/4 cup cooking water.

2. Meanwhile, in dry nonstick 12-inch skillet, cook coconut over medium heat, stirring constantly, until lightly browned, about 3 minutes; transfer to small bowl.

3. In same skillet, heat oil over medium heat until hot; add onion and cook 5 minutes. Add mustard seeds, cumin, coriander, and ground red pepper; cover and cook, shaking skillet frequently, until onion is tender and lightly browned and seeds start to pop, 5 minutes longer.

4. Spoon cauliflower mixture into skillet. Add tomatoes, peas, salt, and reserved cooking water; heat through. Sprinkle with cilantro to serve.

Each serving: About 230 calories, 8g protein, 43g carbohydrate, 4g total fat (1g saturated), 0mg cholesterol, 735mg sodium.

Vegetarian Phyllo Pizza

Delicate layers of phyllo form the crust of this rich, savory pizza.

PREP: 10 MINUTES   BAKE: 15 MINUTES
MAKES 4 MAIN-DISH SERVINGS.

6 sheets (17" by 12" each) fresh or
  frozen (thawed) phyllo
2 tablespoons butter or margarine,
  melted
4 ounces soft, mild goat cheese such
  as Montrâchet

1 jar (6 ounces) marinated artichoke
  hearts, drained and cut into
  1/4-inch pieces
1 1/2 cups grape or cherry tomatoes,
  each cut in half

1. Preheat oven to 450°F. Place 1 sheet of phyllo on ungreased large cookie sheet; brush with some melted butter. Repeat layering with remaining phyllo and butter. Do not brush top layer.
2. Crumble goat cheese over phyllo; top with artichokes and tomatoes. Bake pizza until golden brown around the edges, 12 to 15 minutes.
3. Transfer pizza to large cutting board. With pizza cutter or knife, cut pizza lengthwise in half, then cut each half crosswise into 4 pieces.

Each serving: About 245 calories, 8g protein, 20g carbohydrate, 19g total fat (9g saturated), 29mg cholesterol, 387mg sodium.

Vegetarian Phyllo Pizza

Falafel Cones

Falafel is a staple of Middle Eastern cuisine. It is typically served as a snack or part of an appetizer plate.

PREP: 15 MINUTES   COOK: 10 MINUTES
MAKES 4 MAIN-DISH SERVINGS.

2 cans (15 to 19 ounces each) low-sodium garbanzo beans, rinsed and well drained
2 garlic cloves, peeled
1 large egg
1 cup loosely packed fresh parsley leaves
1/4 cup tahini (sesame seed paste)
1 tablespoon dried mint leaves
2 teaspoons ground cumin
1/4 teaspoon ground red pepper (cayenne)
1/4 cup vegetable oil
2 plum tomatoes, chopped
1 green onion, trimmed and chopped
1 container (8 ounces) plain low-fat yogurt
1/4 teaspoon salt
4 pocketless pitas, warmed

1. In food processor, with knife blade attached, combine beans, garlic, egg, parsley, tahini, mint, cumin, and ground red pepper and puree until smooth. Shape mixture into sixteen 2-inch balls.

2. In nonstick 12-inch skillet, heat oil over medium-high heat until very hot but not smoking. Add falafel balls and cook, turning frequently, until evenly golden, 10 minutes.

3. Meanwhile, in small bowl, combine tomatoes, green onion, yogurt, and salt and stir until mixed.

4. To serve, shape each pita into a cone; tightly wrap bottom of each with kitchen parchment or foil to help hold its shape and prevent leakage. Fill each cone with 4 falafel balls and top with some yogurt mixture.

Each serving: About 670 calories, 28g protein, 94g carbohydrate, 22g total fat (4g saturated), 57mg cholesterol, 740mg sodium.

Vegetarian Tortilla Pie

Vegetarian Tortilla Pie

This dish can be assembled in a jiffy, thanks to its no-cook filling of canned black beans and corn, prepared salsa, and preshredded Jack cheese. A wedge of iceberg lettuce on the side with our Spicy Tomato Dressing (page 153) adds the missing crunch.

PREP: 8 MINUTES   BAKE: 12 MINUTES
MAKES 4 MAIN-DISH SERVINGS.

1 jar (11 to 12 ounces) medium salsa
1 can (8 ounces) no-salt-added tomato sauce
1 can (15 to 16 ounces) no-salt-added black beans, rinsed and drained
1 can (15 1/4 ounces) no-salt-added whole-kernel corn, drained

1/2 cup packed fresh cilantro leaves
4 (10-inch) low-fat flour tortillas
6 ounces shredded reduced-fat Monterey Jack cheese (1 1/2 cups)
reduced-fat sour cream (optional)

1. Preheat oven to 500°F. Spray 15 1/2" by 10 1/2" jelly-roll pan with non-stick cooking spray.
2. In small bowl, mix salsa and tomato sauce. In medium bowl, mix black beans, corn, and cilantro.
3. Place 1 tortilla in jelly-roll pan. Spread one-third of salsa mixture over tortilla. Top with one-third of bean mixture and one-third of cheese. Repeat layering 2 more times, ending with last tortilla.
4. Bake pie until cheese has melted and filling is hot, 10 to 12 minutes. Serve with reduced-fat sour cream, if you like.

Each serving without sour cream: Abut 440 calories, 25g protein, 65g carbohydrate, 11g total fat (5g saturated), 30mg cholesterol, 820mg sodium.

Queso-Blanco Soft Tacos

These tacos are filled with *queso blanco*, a white cheese that's a bit firmer than mozzarella, so it holds its shape when melted. Don't confuse it with *queso fresco*, a crumbly fresh cow's milk cheese that's found in almost every Latin American country.

PREP: 20 MINUTES   COOK: 5 MINUTES
MAKES 4 MAIN-DISH SERVINGS.

3 green onions, trimmed and thinly sliced

3 plum tomatoes, cut into 1/2-inch pieces

1 ripe avocado, peeled, pitted, and cut into 1/2-inch pieces

1/4 small head romaine lettuce, thinly sliced (2 cups)

1/4 cup loosely packed fresh cilantro leaves

1 cup mild or medium-hot salsa

1 package (12 ounces) queso blanco (Mexican frying cheese), cut into 12 slices

12 (6-inch) corn tortillas, warmed

1 lime, cut into 4 wedges

1. On platter, arrange green onions, tomatoes, avocado, lettuce, and cilantro. Pour salsa into serving bowl.

2. Heat nonstick 12-inch skillet over medium-high heat until hot. Add cheese and heat, turning once, until dark brown in spots, 2 to 3 minutes.

3. Place 1 cheese slice in each tortilla and fold in half. Serve tortillas immediately, adding green onions, tomatoes, avocado, lettuce, cilantro, salsa, and a squeeze of lime juice.

Each serving: About 545 calories, 26g protein, 49g carbohydrate, 29g total fat (13g saturated), 60mg cholesterol, 1,300mg sodium.

Queso–Blanco Soft Tacos

ONE-DISH MEALS

Gazpacho-Style Pasta
recipe on page 135

Middle-Eastern Garbanzo Beans and Macaroni

A flavorful stew of pantry staples—canned beans and crushed tomatoes—tossed with pasta makes a satisfying vegetarian entrée.

PREP: 10 MINUTES   COOK: 35 MINUTES
MAKES ABOUT 8 CUPS OR 6 MAIN-DISH SERVINGS.

12 ounces macaroni twists or elbow
  macaroni
1 tablespoon olive oil
1 tablespoon butter or margarine
1 large onion (12 ounces), cut into
  1/4-inch pieces
2 garlic cloves, crushed with
  garlic press
1 teaspoon salt
1 teaspoon ground cumin

3/4 teaspoon ground coriander
1/4 teaspoon ground allspice
1/4 teaspoon coarsely ground
  black pepper
1 can (28 ounces) crushed tomatoes
1 can (15 to 19 ounces) garbanzo
  beans, rinsed and drained
1/4 cup loosely packed fresh parsley
  leaves, chopped
parsley sprigs for garnish

1. In large saucepot, cook pasta as label directs.

2. Meanwhile, in nonstick 12-inch skillet, heat oil with butter over medium heat until hot and melted. Add onion and cook, stirring occasionally, until tender and golden, about 20 minutes. Stir in garlic, salt, cumin, coriander, allspice, and pepper; cook 1 minute.

3. Add tomatoes and garbanzo beans to skillet; heat to boiling over medium-high heat. Reduce heat to medium-low; simmer, stirring occasionally, 5 minutes.

4. Drain pasta; return to saucepot. Toss garbanzo-bean mixture with pasta; heat through. Toss with chopped parsley just before serving. Garnish with parsley sprigs.

Each serving: About 400 calories, 14g protein, 73g carbohydrate, 7g total fat (2g saturated), 5mg cholesterol, 1,039mg sodium.

Middle-Eastern Garbanzo Beans and Macaroni

Lentil Shepherd's Pie

A steaming skillet of Indian-spiced lentils are topped with piping-hot curried mashed sweet potatoes for this nonmeat takeoff on an old comfort-food favorite.

PREP: 20 MINUTES   COOK: 35 MINUTES
MAKES 4 MAIN-DISH SERVINGS.

1 cup dry lentils, rinsed
1 tablespoon grated, peeled
   fresh ginger
1 teaspoon ground cumin
1 can (14 1/2 ounces) vegetable broth
   (1 3/4 cups)
1 bay leaf
2 cups water
1 tablespoon olive oil

1 teaspoon curry powder
1/8 teaspoon crushed red pepper
3 large sweet potatoes (about
   2 pounds), peeled and cut into
   1-inch pieces
1 teaspoon salt
2 green onions, trimmed and
   thinly sliced
plain yogurt (optional)

1. In 12-inch skillet, combine lentils, ginger, cumin, broth, bay leaf, and 1 1/4 cups water; heat to boiling over high heat. Reduce heat to medium; cover and cook until lentils are tender, about 20 minutes. Discard bay leaf.

2. Meanwhile, in 3-quart saucepan, heat oil over medium-high heat until hot. Add curry powder and red pepper and cook, stirring, 15 seconds; add sweet potatoes, salt, and remaining 3/4 cup water; heat to boiling. Reduce heat to medium-low; cover and cook, stirring occasionally, until potatoes are tender, about 15 minutes.

3. With potato masher or fork, mash potato mixture until almost smooth. Spoon mashed potatoes over lentil mixture in skillet; sprinkle with green onions. Serve with yogurt, if you like.

Each serving: About 410 calories, 18g protein, 77g carbohydrate, 5g total fat (1g saturated) 0mg cholesterol, 1,040mg sodium.

Microwave Tomato-Basil Risotto

You don't have to stand at the stove and stir, stir, stir to prepare this risotto—it's cooked in the microwave.

PREP: 5 MINUTES COOK: 25 MINUTES
MAKES 4 MAIN-DISH SERVINGS.

3 1/2 cups vegetable broth
1/2 cup dry white wine
3/4 cup loosely packed fresh
  basil leaves
1 tablespoon olive oil
1 medium shallot, minced
2 cups Arborio rice (Italian short-
  grain rice) or medium-grain rice

3 medium tomatoes (8 ounces each)
3/4 teaspoon salt
1/4 teaspoon coarsely ground
  black pepper
1/2 cup freshly grated Parmesan
  cheese

1. In covered 2-quart saucepan, heat broth and wine over high heat until bubbles form around edge of pan. Meanwhile, coarsely chop basil.

2. In 3 1/2- to 4-quart microwave-safe casserole or bowl, combine oil, shallot, and 1/4 cup chopped basil. Cook, uncovered, in microwave oven on High until shallot has softened, about 1 minute. Add rice and stir until rice grains are opaque. Cook on High 1 minute.

3. Stir hot broth into rice in casserole. Cover and cook on Medium (50% power), stirring once, until most of liquid has been absorbed, about 15 minutes. Meanwhile, chop tomatoes.

4. Stir tomatoes, salt, and pepper into rice mixture. Cover and cook on High, stirring once, until rice is tender but still firm, 3 to 4 minutes. Stir in Parmesan and remaining chopped basil.

Each serving: About 550 calories, 15g protein, 97g carbohydrate, 8g total fat (3g saturated), 8mg cholesterol, 1,490mg sodium.

Editor's Note

This recipe was tested in an 1,100-watt microwave oven. If your microwave has more or less power, it may be necessary to adjust the cooking time.

Carrot Risotto

Carrot Risotto

This quick microwave risotto gets its lovely color and great flavor from shredded carrots and carrot juice.

PREP: 10 MINUTES   COOK: 25 MINUTES
MAKES ABOUT 6 CUPS OR 4 MAIN-DISH SERVINGS.

1 can or bottle (12 to 15 ounces) carrot juice plus enough water to equal 2 cups
1 can (14 1/2 ounces) vegetable broth (1 3/4 cups)
1/2 cup dry white wine
1 1/4 cups water
1 tablespoon olive oil
2 cups shredded carrots

1/2 small onion, finely chopped
2 cups Arborio rice (Italian short-grain rice) or medium-grain rice
1/3 cup freshly grated Parmesan cheese
3/4 teaspoon salt
1/4 teaspoon ground black pepper
2 tablespoons coarsely chopped fresh mint or parsley (optional)

1. In 2-quart saucepan, heat carrot juice, broth, wine, and water to boiling over high heat. Reduce heat to low to maintain simmer; cover.

2. In 3- to 3 1/2-quart microwave-safe casserole, combine oil, carrots, and onion. Cook, uncovered, in microwave oven on High until onion has softened, about 2 minutes. Add rice and stir until rice grains are opaque. Cook on High 1 minute.

3. Stir hot liquid into rice mixture. Cover casserole with lid or vented plastic wrap and cook on Medium (50% power) until most of liquid has been absorbed and rice is tender but still firm, 15 to 20 minutes. Stir in Parmesan, salt, and pepper. Sprinkle with mint, if you like.

Each serving: About 570 calories, 15g protein, 105g carbohydrate, 7g total fat (2g saturated), 7mg cholesterol, 1,110mg sodium.

Couscous Tabbouleh

Instead of the traditional bulgur wheat, this quick tabbouleh is made with couscous. Garbanzo beans add extra protein.

PREP: 20 MINUTES
MAKES 4 MAIN-DISH SERVINGS.

3/4 cup water

3/4 cup couscous

3/4 teaspoon salt

1 can (15 to 19 ounces) garbanzo beans, drained and rinsed

4 medium tomatoes (about 1 1/4 pounds), cut into 1/2-inch pieces

2 Kirby (pickling) cucumbers (about 4 ounces each), unpeeled and cut into 1/2-inch pieces

3/4 cup loosely packed fresh flat-leaf parsley leaves, chopped

1/2 cup loosely packed fresh mint leaves, chopped

1/4 cup fresh lemon juice (from about 2 lemons)

2 tablespoons olive oil

1/4 teaspoon coarsely ground black pepper

1. In microwave-safe 3-quart bowl, heat water to boiling in microwave oven on High, 1 1/2 to 2 minutes. Remove bowl from microwave. Stir in couscous and 1/4 teaspoon salt; cover and let stand until liquid has been absorbed, about 5 minutes.

2. Fluff couscous with fork. Stir in beans, tomatoes, cucumbers, parsley, mint, lemon juice, oil, pepper, and remaining 1/2 teaspoon salt. Serve couscous at room temperature or cover and refrigerate up to 6 hours.

Each serving: About 350 calories, 13g protein, 56g carbohydrate, 9g total fat (1g saturated), 0mg cholesterol, 700mg sodium.

Spaghetti Primavera

A vegetable medley of asparagus, broccoli, and carrots tossed with spaghetti, fresh basil, and Parmesan.

PREP: 20 MINUTES   COOK: 30 MINUTES
MAKES 4 MAIN-DISH SERVINGS.

4 tablespoons butter or margarine
3 medium carrots, cut lengthwise
   into matchstick-thin strips
1 medium onion, chopped
2 garlic cloves, crushed with
   garlic press
salt
1 package (16 ounces) spaghetti
1 bag (16 ounces) broccoli flowerets
1 pound asparagus, trimmed and cut
   diagonally into 1-inch pieces

3/4 teaspoon salt
1/8 to 1/4 teaspoon crushed
   red pepper
1/2 cup water
1 cup loosely packed fresh basil
   leaves, chopped
1/2 cup freshly grated Parmesan
   cheese

1. In nonstick 12-inch skillet, melt 2 tablespoons butter over medium heat. Add carrots and onion and cook, stirring occasionally, until tender and golden, about 10 minutes. Add garlic; cook, stirring, 1 minute.

2. Meanwhile, in large saucepot cook pasta as label directs.

3. To carrot mixture in skillet, add broccoli, asparagus, salt, crushed red pepper, and water; heat to boiling over medium-high heat. Reduce heat to medium; cover and cook, stirring occasionally, until vegetables are tender, 6 to 10 minutes longer.

4. Drain pasta, reserving 3/4 cup pasta water; return pasta to saucepot. Add basil, Parmesan, remaining 2 tablespoons butter, and reserved pasta water; toss well. Add vegetable mixture and gently toss to combine.

Each serving: About 655 calories, 25g protein, 101g carbohydrate, 22g total fat (9g saturated), 39mg cholesterol, 946mg sodium.

Quick-Comfort Egg Noodles and Cabbage

Old-fashioned curly egg noodles are combined with caramelized onion, cabbage, and peas for a cozy family dinner.

PREP: 15 MINUTES   COOK: 30 MINUTES
MAKES 4 MAIN-DISH SERVINGS.

1 package (12 ounces) curly wide egg noodles
1 tablespoon butter or margarine
1 tablespoon olive oil
1 jumbo onion (1 pound), thinly sliced
1 small head (about 1¹/₄ pounds) savoy cabbage, thinly sliced, with tough ribs discarded
1 teaspoon fresh thyme leaves or ¹/₄ teaspoon dried thyme

³/₄ teaspoon salt
¹/₄ teaspoon coarsely ground black pepper
1 package (10 ounces) frozen peas
1 cup vegetable broth
¹/₄ cup freshly grated Parmesan cheese
thyme sprigs for garnish

1. In large saucepot, cook pasta as label directs.
2. Meanwhile, in nonstick 12-inch skillet, heat butter and oil over medium heat until melted and hot. Add onion and cook, stirring occasionally, until onion is tender and golden, about 20 minutes. Increase heat to medium-high; add cabbage, thyme, salt, and pepper and cook, stirring occasionally, until cabbage is tender-crisp and golden, 5 minutes. Stir in frozen peas and broth; cook, stirring, 2 minutes.
3. Drain noodles; return to saucepot. Add cabbage mixture and Parmesan; toss well. Garnish with thyme sprigs.

Each serving: About 540 calories, 22g protein, 88g carbohydrate, 13g total fat (4g saturated), 93mg cholesterol, 1,041mg sodium.

Quick-Comfort Egg Noodles and Cabbage

Lasagna Toss with Spinach and Ricotta

Lasagna Toss with Spinach and Ricotta

This recipe has all the flavor of a layered and baked lasagna, without the wait! Lasagna noodles are tossed with a speedy tomato-spinach skillet sauce, then dolloped with ricotta cheese to serve.

PREP: 20 MINUTES   COOK: 35 MINUTES
MAKES 4 MAIN-DISH SERVINGS.

- 1 package (16 ounces) lasagna noodles
- 1 tablespoon olive oil
- 1 medium onion, finely chopped
- 2 garlic cloves, crushed with garlic press
- 1 can (28 ounces) plum tomatoes
- 3/4 teaspoon salt
- 1/4 teaspoon coarsely ground black pepper
- 1 package (10 ounces) frozen chopped spinach
- 1/2 cup loosely packed fresh basil leaves, chopped
- 1/4 cup freshly grated Parmesan cheese, plus additional for serving (optional)
- 1 cup part-skim ricotta cheese

1. In large saucepot, cook lasagna noodles as label directs, increasing cooking time to 12 to 14 minutes.

2. Meanwhile, in nonstick 12-inch skillet, heat oil over medium heat until hot. Add onion and cook, stirring occasionally, until tender, about 10 minutes. Add garlic and cook, stirring, 30 seconds.

3. Stir in tomatoes with their juice, salt, and pepper, breaking up tomatoes with side of spoon; heat to boiling over high heat. Reduce heat to medium and cook, uncovered, 8 minutes. Add frozen spinach and cook, covered, until spinach is tender, about 10 minutes, stirring occasionally. Stir in basil.

4. Drain noodles; return to saucepot. Add tomato mixture and Parmesan; toss well. Spoon into 4 pasta bowls; top with dollops of ricotta cheese. Serve with additional Parmesan, if you like.

Each serving: About 620 calories, 28g protein, 100g carbohydrate, 12g total fat (5g saturated), 23mg cholesterol, 1,640mg sodium.

Bow Ties with Butternut Squash and Peas

This vegetarian main dish of pasta tossed with butternut squash, peas, and a creamy Parmesan sauce makes a great family dinner. For a low-fat version, use fat-free half-and-half.

PREP: 20 MINUTES   COOK: 15 MINUTES
MAKES 6 MAIN-DISH SERVINGS.

1 package (16 ounces) bow-tie or corkscrew pasta
1 medium butternut squash (2 1/4 pounds), peeled, seeded, and cut into 1-inch pieces
1 package (10 ounces) frozen peas
3/4 cup half-and-half or light cream

1 teaspoon minced fresh sage leaves
1/3 cup freshly grated Parmesan cheese
1 teaspoon salt
1/4 teaspoon coarsely ground black pepper

1. In large saucepot, cook pasta as label directs. Drain.
2. Meanwhile, place squash chunks in 2 1/2-quart microwave-safe baking dish; cover and cook in microwave oven on High, stirring once, 12 minutes. Stir in peas, half-and-half, and sage and cook, uncovered, 2 minutes.
3. In large warm serving bowl, toss pasta with squash mixture, Parmesan, salt, and pepper.

Each serving: About 430 calories, 16g protein, 78g carbohydrate, 7g total fat (3g saturated), 15mg cholesterol, 650mg sodium.

Bow Ties with Butternut Squash and Peas

Gazpacho-Style Pasta

Gazpacho-Style Pasta

Classic gazpacho soup ingredients get pulsed in the food processor while the small seashell pasta cooks. Serve with soup spoons!

PREP: 15 MINUTES   COOK: 15 MINUTES
MAKES 4 MAIN-DISH SERVINGS.

1 package (16 ounces) small shell or orecchiette pasta

1 English (seedless) cucumber (about 1 pound), unpeeled and cut into 2-inch pieces

1/2 medium yellow pepper, cut into 1-inch pieces

1/2 medium red pepper, cut into 1-inch pieces

1/2 medium red onion, cut into 1-inch pieces

1 jalapeño chile, seeded and cut into 1/2-inch pieces

1 garlic clove, cut into thirds

1 1/2 pounds tomatoes (about 5 medium), cut into 1/2-inch pieces

2 tablespoons olive oil

2 tablespoons sherry or red wine vinegar

1 1/2 teaspoons salt

1 small bunch fresh parsley, stems discarded

cucumber slices and cherry tomatoes for garnish

1. In large saucepot, cook pasta as label directs. Drain.

2. Meanwhile, in food processor, with knife blade attached, finely chop cucumber, peppers, onion, chile, and garlic. Do *not* puree.

3. In large serving bowl, toss vegetable mixture with tomatoes, oil, vinegar, and salt until well mixed. Set aside 4 parsley leaves for garnish; chop remaining parsley.

4. Add pasta and chopped parsley to vegetable mixture; toss well to combine. Garnish each serving with cucumber slices, cherry tomatoes, and reserved parsley leaves.

Each serving: About 555 calories, 18g protein, 100g carbohydrate, 9g total fat (1g saturated), 0mg cholesterol, 1,045mg sodium.

Pasta with No-Cook Tomato and Bocconcini Sauce

Bocconcini (Italian for "little mouthfuls") are small balls of mozzarella that can be found packed in whey or water in gourmet shops and in the dairy case of some supermarkets. Sometimes they have been tossed with herbs such as basil and black and crushed red pepper. In this case adjust the seasonings that are called for accordingly.

PREP: 20 MINUTES PLUS STANDING   COOK: 15 MINUTES
MAKES 6 MAIN-DISH SERVINGS.

- 2 pints cherry tomatoes, each cut in half
- 1/2 cup loosely packed fresh flat-leaf parsley leaves, chopped
- 1/2 cup loosely packed fresh basil leaves, thinly sliced
- 1/4 cup olive oil
- 1 teaspoon salt
- 1/4 teaspoon coarsely ground black pepper
- 1 garlic clove, crushed with garlic press
- 1 package (16 ounces) penne or corkscrew pasta
- 12 ounces small mozzarella balls (bocconcini), each cut in half

1. In large serving bowl, stir cherry tomatoes, parsley, basil, oil, salt, pepper, and garlic. Let stand at room temperature at least 1 hour or up to 4 hours to blend flavors.
2. In large saucepot, cook pasta as label directs. Drain well.
3. Add pasta to tomato mixture; toss with bocconcini.

Each serving: About 545 calories, 21g protein, 64g carbohydrate, 23g total fat (9g saturated), 44mg cholesterol, 540mg sodium.

Pasta with No-Cook Tomato and Bocconcini Sauce

Lo Mein with Tofu, Snow Peas, and Carrots

Lo Mein with Tofu, Snow Peas, and Carrots

Lo mein is a Chinese dish of boiled noodles that are stir-fried with any number of vegetables and tofu or other protein and tossed with a soy-based sauce. We've sped up the process with ramen and stir-fry sauce.

PREP: 15 MINUTES   COOK: 15 MINUTES
MAKES 4 MAIN-DISH SERVINGS.

2 packages (3 ounces each) Oriental-flavor ramen noodle soup mix

2 teaspoons vegetable oil

1 package (14 to 15 ounces) extrafirm tofu, patted dry and cut into 1/2-inch cubes

6 ounces snow peas, strings removed and each cut diagonally in half (about 2 cups)

3 green onions, trimmed and cut into 2-inch pieces

1 1/2 cups shredded carrots

1/2 cup bottled stir-fry sauce

3 ounces fresh bean sprouts (about 1 cup), rinsed and drained

1. In 4-quart saucepan, cook ramen noodles (reserve flavor packets) 2 minutes. Drain noodles, reserving 1/4 cup noodle water.

2. Meanwhile, in nonstick 12-inch skillet, heat oil over medium-high heat until very hot. Add tofu and cook, stirring occasionally, until lightly browned, 5 to 6 minutes. Add snow peas and green onions; cook, stirring frequently (stir-frying), until vegetables are tender-crisp, 3 to 5 minutes. Stir in the carrots, stir-fry sauce, and contents of 1 flavor packet to taste (depending on salt level of sauce) and cook until carrots are tender, about 2 minutes. (Discard remaining flavor packet or reserve for another use.)

3. Reserve some bean sprouts for garnish. Add noodles, reserved noodle water, and remaining bean sprouts to skillet; cook, stirring, 1 minute to blend flavors. Sprinkle with reserved bean sprouts to serve.

Each serving: About 375 calories, 18g protein, 47g carbohydrate, 12g total fat (3g saturated), 0mg cholesterol, 1,485mg sodium.

Sesame Noodles

Sesame Noodles

A peanut butter and sesame dressing spiked with orange juice makes this Chinese restaurant–style pasta a favorite with kids as well as adults.

PREP: 15 MINUTES   COOK: 15 MINUTES
MAKES 6 MAIN-DISH SERVINGS.

1 package (16 ounces) spaghetti
1 cup fresh orange juice
1/4 cup seasoned rice vinegar
1/4 cup soy sauce
1/4 cup creamy peanut butter
1 tablespoon Asian sesame oil
1 tablespoon grated, peeled fresh ginger
2 teaspoons sugar
1/4 teaspoon crushed red pepper

1 bag (10 ounces) shredded carrots (about 3 1/2 cups)
3 Kirby cucumbers (about 4 ounces each), unpeeled and cut into 2" by 1/4" matchstick strips
2 green onions, trimmed and thinly sliced
2 tablespoons sesame seeds, toasted (optional)
green onions for garnish

1. In large saucepot, cook pasta as label directs.

2. Meanwhile, in medium bowl, with wire whisk or fork, mix orange juice, vinegar, soy sauce, peanut butter, oil, ginger, sugar, and crushed red pepper until blended; set aside.

3. Place carrots in colander; drain pasta over carrots. In large warm serving bowl, toss pasta mixture, cucumbers, and sliced green onions with peanut sauce. If you like, sprinkle pasta with sesame seeds. Garnish with green onions.

Each serving: About 445 calories, 15g protein, 76g carbohydrate, 9g total fat (2g saturated), 0mg cholesterol, 1,135mg sodium.

Spinach and Rice Frittata

Rice, spinach, and cottage cheese mixed up with mostly egg whites make a delicious, fluffy omelet dinner. Using leftover rice cuts down on prep time, but if you don't have any, cook 1/2 cup raw rice according to package directions.

PREP: 20 MINUTES   BAKE: 20 MINUTES
MAKES 4 MAIN-DISH SERVINGS.

2 teaspoons olive oil
1 medium onion, sliced
8 large egg whites (1 cup, see Tip page 148)
2 large eggs
1 package (10 ounces) frozen chopped spinach, thawed and squeezed dry

1 1/2 cups leftover cooked long-grain white rice
1 container (8 ounces) low-fat cottage cheese (1%)
1/3 cup nonfat (skim) milk
1/4 cup grated Romano cheese
1/2 teaspoon salt
1/8 teaspoon ground black pepper

1. Preheat oven to 425°F. In oven-safe nonstick 10-inch skillet (if skillet is not oven-safe, wrap handle with double layer of foil), heat oil over medium heat until hot. Add onion and cook, covered, until tender and golden, about 8 minutes, stirring occasionally.
2. Meanwhile, in large bowl, with fork, stir egg whites, whole eggs, spinach, rice, cottage cheese, milk, Romano, salt, and pepper until blended.
3. Stir egg mixture into onion in skillet and place in oven. Bake until frittata is set in center, 18 to 20 minutes. Cut into wedges to serve.

Each serving: About 265 calories, 23g protein, 25g carbohydrate, 7g total fat (2g saturated), 114mg cholesterol, 830mg sodium.

Egg and Black Bean Burritos

Scrambled eggs with a sprinkling of Monterey Jack are wrapped in flour tortillas with black beans and salsa—like the popular takeout but better—and it's on the table in just 15 minutes!

PREP: 10 MINUTES   COOK: 5 MINUTES
MAKES 4 MAIN-DISH SERVINGS.

1 can (15 to 19 ounces) black beans, rinsed and drained
1 jar (11 ounces) medium-hot salsa (about 1¼ cups)
6 large eggs
¼ teaspoon salt

⅛ teaspoon coarsely ground black pepper
4 ounces shredded Monterey Jack cheese (1 cup)
4 (10-inch) flour tortillas

1. In small microwave-safe bowl, mix black beans with salsa; set aside. In medium bowl, with wire whisk or fork, beat eggs, salt, and black pepper until blended.

2. Heat nonstick 10-inch skillet over medium-high heat until hot. Add egg mixture to skillet. As egg mixture begins to set around edge, stir lightly with heat-safe rubber spatula or wooden spoon to allow uncooked egg mixture to flow toward side of pan. Continue cooking until edges are set to desired doneness, about 5 minutes. Remove skillet from heat; sprinkle cheese evenly over eggs.

3. Meanwhile, in microwave oven, heat black-bean mixture on High, stirring once, until heated through, 1 to 2 minutes. Cover and keep warm.

4. Stack tortillas and place between 2 damp microwave-safe paper towels. In microwave oven, heat tortillas on High until warm, about 1 minute.

5. For each burrito, place one-fourth of scrambled eggs down center of 1 tortilla; top with about one-fourth of black-bean mixture. Fold two opposing sides of tortilla over filling, then fold over remaining sides to form a package.

Each serving: About 575 calories, 28g protein, 71g carbohydrate, 21g total fat (9g saturated), 344mg cholesterol, 1,550mg sodium.

Corn and Jack Quesadillas

Corn and Jack Quesadillas

After a bite of one of these quesadillas, you'll agree that taking the time to grill fresh ears of corn and then cut the kernels from the cob was well worth it. If you're grilling dinner the day before you serve these, you can grill the corn ahead and refrigerate it for even easier prep.

PREP: 10 MINUTES PLUS COOLING   GRILL: 11 MINUTES
MAKES 4 MAIN-DISH SERVINGS.

3 large ears corn, husks and silks removed

4 (8- to 10-inch) low-fat flour tortillas

4 ounces reduced-fat Monterey Jack cheese, shredded (1 cup)

1/2 cup mild or medium-hot salsa

2 green onions, trimmed and thinly sliced

1 head romaine lettuce, thinly sliced

1 tablespoon olive oil

1 tablespoon cider vinegar

1/2 teaspoon coarsely ground black pepper

1/4 teaspoon salt

1. Prepare grill.

2. Place corn on hot grill rack over medium–high heat. Cover grill and cook corn, turning frequently, until brown in spots, 10 to 15 minutes. Transfer corn to plate; set aside until cool enough handle. With sharp knife, cut kernels from cobs.

3. Place tortillas on work surface. Evenly divide Monterey Jack, salsa, green onions, and corn on half of each tortilla. Fold tortilla over filling to make 4 quesadillas.

4. Place quesadillas on hot grill rack. Grill quesadillas, turning once, until browned on both sides, 1 to 2 minutes. Transfer quesadillas to cutting board; cut each into 3 pieces.

5. In large bowl, toss romaine with oil, vinegar, pepper, and salt. Serve quesadillas with romaine salad.

Each serving: About 330 calories, 16g protein, 47g carbohydrate, 11g total fat (5g saturated), 20mg cholesterol, 940mg sodium.

Tomato and Cheese Pie

Tomato and Cheese Pie

A savory custard pie that bakes right in the pie plate—with no crust!

PREP: 20 MINUTES BAKE: 35 MINUTES
MAKES 6 MAIN-DISH SERVINGS.

1 container (15 ounces) part-skim
  ricotta cheese
4 large eggs
1/4 cup freshly grated Parmesan
  cheese
3/4 teaspoon salt plus additional for
  sprinkling
1/8 teaspoon coarsely ground black
  pepper plus additional for sprinkling

1/4 cup low-fat milk (1%)
1 tablespoon cornstarch
1 cup packed fresh basil leaves,
  chopped
1 pound ripe tomatoes (about
  3 medium), thinly sliced

1. Preheat oven to 375°F. In large bowl, with wire whisk or fork, beat ricotta, eggs, Parmesan, salt, and pepper until blended.

2. In cup, with fork, stir milk and cornstarch until blended; whisk into cheese mixture. Stir in basil. Pour mixture into 9-inch glass or ceramic pie plate. Arrange tomatoes on top, overlapping if necessary. Sprinkle tomatoes with salt and pepper.

3. Bake pie until lightly browned around edge and center is puffed, 30 to 35 minutes.

Each serving: About 190 calories, 15g protein, 10g carbohydrate, 10g total fat (5g saturated), 167mg cholesterol, 515mg sodium.

Moroccan-Spiced Sweet-Potato Medley

A spicy combination of vegetables cooked with bulgur and sweetened with dark raisins.

PREP: 20 MINUTES   COOK: 30 MINUTES
MAKES 4 MAIN-DISH SERVINGS.

2 teaspoons olive oil
1 medium onion, sliced
2 garlic cloves, crushed with garlic press
1 1/2 teaspoons ground coriander
1 1/2 teaspoons ground cumin
1 teaspoon salt
1/4 teaspoon ground red pepper (cayenne)
1 1/2 pounds sweet potatoes (about 2 medium), peeled and cut into 3/4-inch pieces

1 can (14 1/2 ounces) stewed tomatoes
1 cup bulgur (cracked wheat)
2 1/4 cups water
1 can (15 to 19 ounces) garbanzo beans, drained and rinsed
1/2 cup dark seedless raisins
1 cup loosely packed fresh cilantro leaves, chopped
plain low-fat yogurt (optional)

1. In nonstick 12-inch skillet, heat oil over medium heat until hot. Add onion and cook, covered, stirring occasionally, until tender and golden, about 8 minutes. Add garlic, coriander, cumin, salt, and ground red pepper and cook, stirring, 1 minute.

2. Add the potatoes, tomatoes, bulgur, and water; heat to boiling over medium-high heat. Reduce heat to medium-low; cover and simmer until potatoes are fork-tender, about 20 minutes. Stir in beans, raisins, and cilantro; heat through. Serve with yogurt, if you like.

Each serving: About 525 calories, 16g protein, 109g carbohydrate, 5g total fat (1g saturated), 0mg cholesterol, 1,080mg sodium.

Moroccan-Spiced Sweet-Potato Medley

Grilled Tomato and Basil Pizzas

Grilled Tomato and Basil Pizzas

Garden tomatoes and basil make a wonderful topping for pizza cooked over the coals. For the crust, use frozen bread dough or fresh dough from the supermarket or pizzeria.

PREP: 30 MINUTES   GRILL: 6 TO 9 MINUTES PER PIZZA
MAKES 4 PIZZAS OR 4 MAIN-DISH SERVINGS.

1 pound (1 piece) frozen bread
  dough, thawed (from 2- to 3-pound
  package)
2 tablespoons olive oil
4 ripe medium tomatoes (about 1½
  pounds), sliced
4 ounces fresh mozzarella cheese,
  sliced, or 1 cup shredded Fontina
  cheese

½ teaspoon salt
½ teaspoon ground black pepper
1 cup loosely packed fresh basil
  leaves, chopped, plus additional
  leaves for garnish

1. Prepare grill.
2. Cut thawed bread dough into 4 pieces. On oiled cookie sheet, spread and flatten 1 piece of dough to ⅛-inch thickness. Lightly brush dough with some oil. On same cookie sheet, repeat with another piece of dough. Repeat with another oiled cookie sheet and remaining pieces of dough. For easiest handling, cover and refrigerate dough on cookie sheets until ready to use.
3. Place 1 piece of dough at a time, greased side down, on grill over medium-low heat. Grill until dough stiffens (dough may puff slightly) and grill marks appear on underside, 2 to 3 minutes. Brush top with some oil.
4. With tongs, turn crust over. Quickly top with one-fourth of tomatoes and one-fourth of cheese. Cook pizza until cheese melts and underside is evenly browned and cooked through, 4 to 6 minutes longer.
5. With tongs, transfer pizza to cutting board. Sprinkle pizza with ⅛ teaspoon salt and ⅛ teaspoon pepper. Scatter one-fourth of chopped basil on pizza and garnish with basil leaves. Drizzle with some oil, if you like. Serve immediately.
6. Repeat with remaining dough and toppings.

Each serving: About 495 calories, 18g protein, 63g carbohydrate, 20g total fat (7g saturated), 34mg cholesterol, 1,175mg sodium.

Whole-Wheat Pita Pizzas with Vegetables

Whole-Wheat Pita Pizzas with Vegetables

We topped whole-wheat pitas with ricotta cheese, garbanzo beans, and sautéed vegetables for a fast dinner the whole family will love.

PREP: 25 MINUTES   BAKE: 13 MINUTES
MAKES 8 PIZZAS OR 4 MAIN-DISH SERVINGS.

1 teaspoon olive oil
1 medium red onion, sliced
2 garlic cloves, crushed with garlic
   press
1/4 teaspoon crushed red pepper
8 ounces broccoli flowerets, cut into
   1 1/2-inch pieces
1/2 teaspoon salt
1/4 cup water

1 can (15 to 19 ounces) garbanzo
   beans, rinsed and drained
1 cup part-skim ricotta cheese
4 (6-inch) whole-wheat pitas, split
   horizontally in half
1/2 cup freshly grated Parmesan
   cheese
2 medium plum tomatoes, cut into
   1/2-inch pieces

1. Preheat oven to 450°F. In nonstick 12-inch skillet, heat oil over medium-high heat until hot. Add onion and cook, stirring occasionally, until golden, 7 to 10 minutes. Add garlic and crushed red pepper, and cook, stirring, 30 seconds. Add broccoli flowerets, 1/4 teaspoon salt, and water; heat to boiling. Reduce heat to medium and cook, covered, until broccoli is tender-crisp, about 5 minutes.

2. Meanwhile, in small bowl, with potato masher or fork, mash beans with ricotta and remaining 1/4 teaspoon salt until almost smooth.

3. Arrange pita halves on 2 large cookie sheets. Bake until lightly toasted, about 3 minutes. Spread bean mixture on toasted pitas. Top with broccoli mixture and sprinkle with Parmesan. Bake until heated through, 7 to 10 minutes longer. Sprinkle with tomatoes to serve. Serve 2 rounds per person.

Each serving: About 510 calories, 27g protein, 77g carbohydrate, 13g total fat (6g saturated), 27mg cholesterol, 1,155mg sodium.

Polenta with Spicy Eggplant Sauce

A great dinner you can whip up after you get home from work: Polenta cooks in the microwave oven with minimal attention while you prepare a quick skillet sauce.

PREP: 15 MINUTES   COOK: 25 MINUTES
MAKES 4 MAIN-DISH SERVINGS.

1 tablespoon olive oil
1 medium onion, finely chopped
2 small eggplants (about 1 pound each), cut into 1-inch pieces
1 garlic clove, crushed with garlic press
1/4 teaspoon crushed red pepper

1 can (28 ounces) crushed tomatoes
1 1/2 teaspoons salt
2 cups low-fat (1%) milk
1 1/2 cups yellow cornmeal
Parmesan-cheese wedge for garnish (optional)

1. In nonstick 12-inch skillet, heat oil over medium heat until hot. Add onion and cook, stirring occasionally, 5 minutes. Increase heat to medium-high; add eggplant and cook, stirring occasionally, until golden and tender, about 8 minutes. Add garlic and crushed red pepper and cook, stirring, 1 minute. Add tomatoes, 1/2 teaspoon salt, and *1/2 cup water;* heat to boiling. Reduce heat to low; cover and simmer, stirring occasionally, 10 minutes.

2. Meanwhile, in deep 4-quart microwave-safe bowl or casserole, combine milk, cornmeal, 1 teaspoon salt, and *4 1/2 cups water.* Cook in microwave oven on High until thickened, 15 to 20 minutes. After the first 5 minutes of cooking, whisk vigorously until smooth (mixture will be lumpy at first), and twice more during remaining cooking time.

3. While polenta is cooking, with vegetable peeler, remove long, thin strips from Parmesan wedge for garnish, if you like.

4. To serve, spoon polenta into 4 bowls; top with eggplant sauce. Garnish each serving with some Parmesan strips if using.

Each serving: About 380 calories, 13g protein, 71g carbohydrate, 6g total fat (2g saturated), 5mg cholesterol, 1,235mg sodium.

Polenta with Spicy Eggplant Sauce

INDEX

METRIC CONVERSION CHARTS

The recipes that appear in this cookbook use the standard United States method for measuring liquid and dry or solid ingredients (teaspoons, tablespoons, and cups). The information on this chart is provided to help cooks outside the U.S. successfully use these recipes. All equivalents are approximate.

METRIC EQUIVALENTS FOR DIFFERENT TYPES OF INGREDIENTS

A standard cup measure of a dry or solid ingredient will vary in weight depending on the type of ingredient. A standard cup of liquid is the same volume for any type of liquid. Use the following chart when converting standard cup measures to grams (weight) or milliliters (volume).

Standard Cup	Fine Powder (e.g. flour)	Grain (e.g. rice)	Granular (e.g. sugar)	Liquid Solids (e.g. butter)	Liquid (e.g. milk)
1	140 g	150 g	190 g	200 g	240 ml
3/4	105 g	113 g	143 g	150 g	180 ml
2/3	93 g	100 g	125 g	133 g	160 ml
1/2	70 g	75 g	95 g	100 g	120 ml
1/3	47 g	50 g	63 g	67 g	80 ml
1/4	35 g	38 g	48 g	50 g	60 ml
1/8	18 g	19 g	24 g	25 g	30 ml

USEFUL EQUIVALENTS FOR LIQUID INGREDIENTS BY VOLUME

1/4 tsp =				1 ml
1/2 tsp =				2 ml
1 tsp =				5 ml
3 tsp =	1 tbls =		1/2 fl oz =	15 ml
	2 tbls =	1/8 cup =	1 fl oz =	30 ml
	4 tbls =	1/4 cup =	2 fl oz =	60 ml
	5 1/3 tbls =	1/3 cup =	3 fl oz =	80 ml
	8 tbls =	1/2 cup =	4 fl oz =	120 ml
	10 2/3 tbls =	2/3 cup =	5 fl oz =	160 ml
	12 tbls =	3/4 cup =	6 fl oz =	180 ml
	16 tbls =	1 cup =	8 fl oz =	240 ml
	1 pt =	2 cups =	16 fl oz =	480 ml
	1 qt =	4 cups =	32 fl oz =	960 ml
			33 fl oz =	1000 ml = 1 l

USEFUL EQUIVALENTS FOR DRY INGREDIENTS BY WEIGHT

(To convert ounces to grams, multiply the number of ounces by 30.)

1 oz =	1/16 lb =			30 g
4 oz =	1/4 lb =			120 g
8 oz =	1/2 lb =			240 g
12 oz =	3/4 lb =			360 g
16 oz =	1 lb =			480 g

USEFUL EQUIVALENTS FOR COOKING/OVEN TEMPERATURES

	Fahrenheit	Celsius	Gas Mark
Freeze Water	32° F	0° C	
Room Temperature	68° F	20° C	
Boil Water	212° F	100° C	
Bake	325° F	160° C	3
	350° F	180° C	4
	375° F	190° C	5
	400° F	200° C	6
	425° F	220° C	7
	450° F	230° C	8
Broil			Grill

USEFUL EQUIVALENTS FOR LENGTH

(To convert inches to centimeters, multiply the number of inches by 2.5.)

1 in =			2.5 cm
6 in =	1/2 ft =		15 cm
12 in =	1 ft =		30 cm
36 in =	3 ft = 1 yd =		90 cm
40 in =			100 cm = 1 m